I Am Not My Body
A Tribute to Jim MacLaren

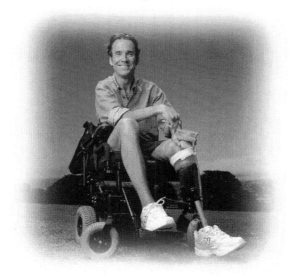

Jennifer Hippensteel

ISBN-13: 978-1726295826

ISBN-10: 1726295826

Printed in the United States by CreateSpace
Available from Amazon.com and other online stores

DEDICATION

In Memory of Bruce Hippensteel

I dedicate this book in memory of my soul mate and
loving husband of twenty-five years.

Bruce Hippensteel
11/22/49–04/08/2018

The loving father of our four exceptional children, Kiowa, Noah, Sage, and
Maya. We shared so very many memories as we grew and expanded
together. Although we were separated in your passing, my love and respect
for you lives on. I will forever carry you in my heart, and I will see you
every time I look at our beautiful children. You are finally "Free Like the
Breeze" my sweet Calvin, and I remain forever your Hobbes.

— Jennifer

CONTENTS

Heroism isn't a one-time thing. Live heroically.

— *Jim Maclaren*

ACKNOWLEDGMENTS

I could never have completed this manuscript without the help of so many.

To my editor and dear Soul Sister, Karal Gregory, I thank you with all my heart for your support and creativity; without you this tribute would never have happened.

To my beautiful friend Dawn Mentzer, freelance writer, for contributing the Foreword, a part of the book I struggled with on my own for far too long.

To my four amazing, talented, and magical children, Kiowa, Noah, Sage, and Maya, thank you for being my joy, and my support system and for choosing me as your earthly Mother. I love you all so very much.

To all of my soul connections that have laughed and cried with me, contributed to this book, and supported me for almost 8 long years now, I thank you.

To William, for your love and beautiful heart.

To the Challenged Athletes Foundation, which was started years ago to buy an accessible van for my brother Jim and continued on to help thousands around the world. They have made it their mission to give people with challenges the ability to engage in life again. Please consider supporting their very important endeavors. www.challengedathletes.org.

Last but not least, to the Universe, for bringing my brother and all of these incredible people into my life.

I am forever blessed.

INTRODUCTION

Jim MacLaren. A man with a spirit that transcends this place we call Earth.

Jim defied death with two traumatic accidents. One took his left leg below the knee and ended his shot at playing professional football. The other paralyzed him from the neck down, landing him forever in a wheelchair. Not one to let life keep him down, he reinvented himself—first as the world's fastest amputee triathlete, competing in Ironman competitions and often beating his able-legged opponents—and then as a motivational speaker and writer, inspiring the world with his positive, courageous attitude. Jim was a pioneer, sent to Earth to live life on his own terms while paving the way for others confronted by seemingly insurmountable odds. His life and courage touched many throughout this world, and his legacy is his story, reminding all of us that life's challenges do not stop us but instead allow us to become the very best we can be.

In 2005, EPSN honored Jim with the Arthur Ashe Courage Award, presented annually to individuals whose contributions transcend sports. In August 2010, 25 years after his first accident, Jim passed away in his sleep at the age of 47. *I Am Not My Body* is an emotional journey through the short but powerful life of Jim MacLaren. Journal entries written by Jim's sister and soulmate throughout the months after her big brother's death, as well as tributes by those Jim inspired and a chapter from his unpublished memoir, allow us to share both her journey as she learned to live without her brother's earthly presence and the life of a most inspiring man.

FOREWORD

In any true-life story filled with emotion, as Jim MacLaren's certainly is, facts are a necessity. They establish context; they provide a frame of reference.

For those of you not yet familiar with Jim's story, I hope this background and the tragic and triumphant milestones of his incredible and incredulous life journey will give you perspective. I regret never having the honor of meeting Jim, but since becoming friends with his sister, Jennifer, he has become a part of my life and a source of inspiration. I believe, by the end of this book, you will feel as though you knew him personally, too.

Jim was gifted. He had it all—brains, brawn, creativity, and athleticism. As a buff 6'5", 300-pound student at Yale University, he excelled at lacrosse and was a standout All-American defensive tackle on the football team. Academically, he more than held his own, and he showed great promise in his acting pursuits at Yale School of Drama. These are not opinions; they are facts.

In October 1985, Jim was driving his motorcycle in New York City when a 40,000-pound New York City bus hit him. The accident cost Jim his left leg below the knee.

Jim reinvented his life after the accident in 1985. He trained with determination and set records as an amputee athlete in the New York City marathon (3:16) and the Ironman Hawaii (10:42). Jim also began his tour as a motivational speaker, inspiring others challenged with disabilities.

While competing in the Orange County Performing Arts Triathlon in Mission Viejo, California in June 1993, Jim met another tragic fate. Officials misjudged his speed on the bike course and allowed a van to cross in front of him. That van struck Jim, propelling him into a signpost. The doctors told him he was a quadriplegic and would never feel anything or move from the chest down for the rest of his life.

Jim defied the odds, tackling rehab with abandon and gaining a degree of motor control and independence the doctors did not think would be possible for him. Much of that was as a result of the generosity of several of his triathlete friends who created the Challenged Athletes Foundation and held the first San Diego Triathlon Challenge, which raised $48,000—$23,000 over the goal of $25,000—to buy Jim a vehicle he could drive with just his hands. Jim resumed his career as a motivational speaker.

All the while, however, he fought to overcome unrelenting depression and pain. Enduring a battle with cocaine addiction, Jim came close to losing everything and everyone. Fortunately, through rehab, renewed focus, and the help of family and friends who would not give up on him, Jim conquered those demons. In 2005, Jim received the Arthur Ashe Courage Award at the annual ESPYS ceremony in Los Angeles.

Jim MacLaren died as a result of complications from an illness on August 31, 2010 at the age of 47. Although he has left us physically, his legacy of humanity and inspiration live on.

You will find this book evidence of that as you read what others have to say about what Jim taught them about facing adversity and making life meaningful, even when it has become something far removed from what you envisioned it would be.

— *Dawn Mentzer*

1 A NOTE FROM KIRK DOUGLAS

August 11, 2015

Dear Jennifer,

I am happy you have written a book about your brother Jim. I have fond memories of Jim MacLaren many years ago. He was an amazing guy who handled his disability with grace and ease. We had many interesting talks. I admire him very much.

Sincerely,

Kirk Douglas

2 JIM'S EULOGY
by Ben Lloyd (Yale School of Drama)

The first thing you say when someone asks you to give a eulogy is "Why me?" The first thing you say when someone asks you to give Jim MacLaren's eulogy is "O my God! Why me?!" After Hillary called me and extended this profound honor to me, I hung up and buried my head in my hands. How to encapsulate the extraordinary drama of Jim's life in fifteen minutes? How to do justice to his accomplishments? How to recognize all the people he touched, and who meant so much to him? Jim, as some of you know, was fond of practical jokes. Or at least, he knew how to have a good laugh at someone else's predicament, so . . . . Thanks, bro. Good one.

So at the outset: thank you Mom, Dad, Step-Dad, Sisters, Brothers. Thank you, Jim's family, for this honor.

So I will tell my story of Jim. And I will leave so much out. So much I don't know about. So much I never knew about him. And so I encourage all of you: tell me what I left out . . . later. Tell each other. Tell your stories of Jim to me and to each other, and to the world,

7

today and for the rest of your lives. Because this is how we honor him now. We are Jim MacLaren's storytellers. And what an amazing story it is. Jim has now become what I think God intended for him to become—a myth. And I don't mean "myth" as in a fiction, something untrue. No. I mean myth the way Joseph Campbell thought of myth: not as a lie, but as a symbol or metaphor for something mysterious, heroic, and true.

The title of my eulogy is a phrase Jim used continually following his second accident: *I Am Not My Body.* I met Jim in 1981 or 82. Jim was recruited by Yale College to play football and lacrosse, and he and I were in the same graduating class, the class of 1985. Although I don't remember the moment, I'm sure that when I first laid eyes on him I had the following thought: "dumb jock." Jim stood six foot four and nearly 275 pounds. He was easy-going, no discernable accent, and had a manner which was decidedly working-class. At a place like Yale, that was noticeable. I was the same basic shape I am now, but probably twenty pounds lighter, and I actually had hair. So my knee-jerk assessment of Jim was as much a product of envy as it was of my late-adolescent tendency to make assumptions about people based on how they look. I wanted to look like him.

But here comes Jim's first lesson to me: I am not my body. I sat in theater classes with Jim and listened to his thoughtful feedback on others' work. I was affected by his gentleness. I was seduced by his smile and sense of humor. I suddenly got it: this guy's full of surprises. Surprising that his responses to the work in class were genuine, and not the rote responses we learn to give when we figure out what teacher is looking for. Surprising that he saw things I didn't see. Surprising that this athletic recruit was in an acting class at all. Surprising how good he was: well prepared, brave on stage, expressive, and not at all stuck in some self-limiting "macho" persona. I can see Jim now, after we got to know each other, over a beer and a slice at Yorkside Pizza, tilting back in his chair, arching an eyebrow and smiling at me: "You thought I was stupid, didn't you Benny?" Yeah, I did Jim. Before I even knew you. But I was the stupid one, because you were not your body.

I loved being around Jim. His size and personality gave him a sparkle that I enjoyed bathing in, hoping it would put me in a better light. He was fun, with a mischievous streak a mile long. Our relationship revolved for the most part around the usual stuff two straight guys in college like to talk about: sex, sports and having fun. But as we got to know each other better, we discovered something deeper we shared in common: the similar circumstances of our families of origin. In a deeply personal way we couldn't possibly describe, Jim and I "got" each other.

James E. Snow was born April 13th, 1963 in Concord, New Hampshire. Later in life, he was legally adopted by his stepfather and his last name was changed to MacLaren. His mom remembers the forceps marks on his face, his full head of hair, and that at birth "he looked like he needed a shave." Needless to say, she was concerned about his future appearance. I think he turned out just fine, Mom. As a baby, Jim smiled early and often, never crawled, and began walking at sixteen months. His family called him Jamie. He adored his grandfather Burt, and his early years were filled with love.

In 1968, he moved with his family to Illinois. In '69 they went to California. In '71, at age eight, his parents divorced and he moved with his mom and siblings back to New Hampshire. He was so big at ten years old that, much to his mom's distress, his school wanted him to play football with the eighth graders. The beating he must have took paid off, because later, he went to the Vermont Academy and became an All-American lacrosse player and football star. He arrived at Yale in the fall of 1981.

Some of my high points with Jim at Yale came working on a scene from a play called *Bent*, about two gay men sent to the concentration camps in World War II. "I want to stretch myself, Benny," Jim told me, "I'm always getting cast as these muscle men and enforcers. I want to work on something really different." What I would have given to have been cast as a muscle man, just once. But, like I said, Jim was full of surprises, so we worked on this scene from *Bent*, as lovers, and we kissed on stage in front of a room full of our peers and one of the scariest acting teachers I ever took a class with. The kiss? It was just a peck. Jim would laugh, smack me on the head after rehearsal and say, "No tongue, dude!"

Or the production of David Mamet's play *Edmond* we were both in our senior year. Somehow, for both of us, this production was a culminating experience. It's an intense, dark, and violent play—just the kind of play two cocky Yalies drunk on testosterone would love. And we loved it. At the time, Jim was a member of a "secret society" (a kind of glorified fraternity at Yale). Like so much else about Jim, I was jealous of his membership in Wolf's Head, but it was one of the only societies that allowed senior class visitors. Some the best times I had with Jim were in the spring of 1985, after rehearsals or performances of *Edmond*, in the basement of Wolf's Head, having the kind of fun it would be rude to describe at an event like this one.

Or the one and only spring break trip I ever took, which I took with Jim. These were the days when credit card companies would send seniors applications and then Visa cards. Jim always had, shall we say, an *enthusiastic* relationship to money. Simply put, if he wanted it, he bought it, whether he had the money or not. Jim never met a credit line he didn't love. So we paid for this trip to Florida with these funny little pieces of plastic, rented a car, and drove to Miami. It was . . . well, you know what it was. Jim got lucky, I didn't, what a surprise. We drove around with a case of light beer in the trunk. We were on top of the world.

Later in the spring of 1985, all of us Theatre Studies majors had a rude awakening. We were about to graduate, and most of us didn't have clue what to do next. So, most of us tried to buy a little extra time by staying in school, and we auditioned for graduate schools in theater. Much to my surprise, I was accepted at the Yale School of Drama. Jim was wait-listed, and we rejoiced, knowing that we would be together again after a year.

That fall I began a very different kind of educational experience at the Drama School, and Jim got on his motorcycle and went to New York, to study and live a little before what was essentially a formality— his re-audition for Yale School of Drama the following spring. On

October 13th, 1985, riding home from an acting class he was taking in Manhattan, Jim was broad-sided by a New York City bus. They chalked the outline of his body on the street, and he was pronounced dead on arrival at the hospital.

But remember, this man was full of surprises. I am not my body, he said.

He came back from the dead. They cut his left leg off below the knee. By January 1986, he was being fitted with a prosthetic and learning to walk again. He re-auditioned on schedule in March, and was accepted to the Yale School of Drama's class of actors to graduate in 1989.

If I think about it, I believe that Jim's deep reverence for life, for the experience of living, began in his recovery from that first accident. Jim carried with him the profound knowledge of *having been dead*, medically speaking. And so he began to see himself as miraculous in the years after he lost his leg. And he was. That first accident also loosed Jim from any conventional design to the trajectory of his life. Sure, he was in drama school, but so what? Life is short, no one knew this more deeply than Jim. So go as you are led, follow your heart, because for Jim it was no joke—you could be run over by a bus tomorrow.

I am not my body, he said. And so, during the three years of his training in drama school, Jim simultaneously began a training of different kind. He began to transform his body: from that of a former defensive lineman, to that of a world-class triathlete. Jim became fascinated by his own body, and at the same time he began to experience it as a limitation, a boundary. And he sought to push the edge of that boundary further and further. If there was ever a sport designed for the phrase "I am not my body" it is the sport of triathlons, in which human beings push themselves beyond any sense of limitation to feats of endurance and physical accomplishment which seem impossible. This was the sport Jim was drawn to. It could have been golf. It could have been archery. No, not for Jim MacLaren. It had to be a big deal. It had to be triathlons.

Looking back, I think there was defiance in it. Looking back, I think somewhere, deep inside, Jim the competitive athlete was saying to God, to the universe, to whoever was watching: Yeah? You wanna take my leg? Fine—go for it. Now watch this. And as he became better and better at it, he began to weave his own myth, which contained the notion that the accident had happened for a reason: so that he could transform himself and excel at endurance sports.

After graduating from the Yale School of Drama with an MFA in Acting, Jim spent a few months in New York, appeared in a soap opera, and then gave in to his passion. He began training full time, quickly found sponsors, and by 1990 was routinely finishing marathons in front of eighty percent of the able-bodied competitors. Jim set world records for disabled marathon runners and triathletes, competed in the legendary Ironman triathlon in Hawaii, was featured in major sports magazines including *Sports Illustrated*, and is in the Triathlon Hall of Fame. I went to New York and bartended. I completely lost touch with Jim from 1988 to 1993.

This is a phenomenon many people experienced with Jim—this

aspect of having him seemingly at the center of your life, then having him nearly disappear. His level of dedication made Jim obsessively focused on his training, and he let nothing get in the way, not even relationships to friends and family. And let's be honest—actors are narcissistic creatures. I should know. Add to an actor the life and training of a world-class triathlete and you have one of the most self-centered people in the world. Not necessarily in a bad sense, I mean, he had to be. But it's also true that Jim wasn't the greatest at returning phone calls and emails. And anyway, who could keep up with him during this time of his life? For me, he became the stuff of second-hand stories I heard from classmates—did you hear about Jim? About his time in that triathlon? About that article about him? And so, even before 1993, Jim was living into his own myth: perhaps it was Jim MacLaren Myth version 1.0. I am not my body, my wounded, one-legged body. No. Look at me now world. I am heroic, superhuman and nearly perfectly fit.

I am not my body.

In June 1993 I was living the actor's rat race in New York and burning out fast. Then my friend—a drama school classmate of Jim's, the actress Mary Mara—called me in tears. She was crying so hard I couldn't understand her. Then I began to understand. Jim had been in another accident. Most of you know the details. But let's listen to Jim tell it:

> The race starts. I finish the mile swim and hop on my bike. A couple miles into the bike ride on a closed course, I'm stretched out on my aerodynamic handlebars, just flying. I assumed the people watching were applauding until I realized they were

screaming. I look over to my left, and coming right at me is the grill of a black van. I learned later that a traffic marshal had misjudged my speed approaching the intersection and had directed the van to cross the street.

Life in these moments really slows down. I remember thinking, *Okay, if I pedal one click faster, I can beat this guy across the intersection.* The last thing I remember hearing is people screaming and the driver hitting his accelerator instead of his brakes. He struck my back wheel, I was thrown from my bike, flew headfirst into a signpost, and broke my neck.

None of that I remember. I woke up in the ambulance, still in race mode, feeling the adrenaline. I was in the same state of mind I had been in eight years earlier—when I first woke up after getting hit by that bus and saw that my leg was missing, I thought, *Oh, okay, cool, your left leg's gone.* And I went back to sleep. When I woke up the day after that, that's when my ego and brain started freaking out.

So when I came to in the ambulance, I knew right away that my legs didn't work. But I remember thinking, *Oh, maybe I'm just a paraplegic. Maybe I'll be able to wheelchair race. And I could go beat Jim Knaub* (who held all the wheelchair marathon records). Then I blacked out again.

The next thing I know, I'm in the hospital, outside the OR. A doctor is holding my hand. He tells me straight, "Look, you're a C5-C6 quad, which means that you broke your neck right up around your ears, and you're never going to move or feel again from the chest down for the rest of your life." At that moment, there was some aspect of me that felt that if he never let go of my hand, that I'd be okay. But, of course, he had to let go because they wheeled me into the OR. That was the start of multiple surgeries and months of being in the ICU. Basically, the inferno had begun.

It was hell.

That's from one of Jim's motivational speeches.

The phrase that went around the drama school community was "It's Greek." It's Greek what happened to Jim. By that we meant, the only way to comprehend what had happened to Jim with this second, unbelievably awful accident, was as if we were witnessing an ancient Greek tragedy, written by Aeschylus or Sophocles. These are plays of curses, miracles, and divine intervention; plays in which the painful and chaotic experience of life is expressed through the drama of heroic characters making heroic choices or facing horrible circumstances. These are mythic plays. At the end, there is always some lesson learned, as if the Greeks are telling us, see? There is a moral to the story.

Except that what happened to Jim was not a play. It was real life. The great challenge we faced with Jim was that, in 1993, we didn't know how the play would end. We knew we were only in the third act—the part of the play when the really bad stuff happens—and that there were still two acts to come.

The next seven years were really, really hard for Jim. This was the time he learned exactly what he would be dealing with, if he chose life. And really, who could have blamed him if he didn't? It seemed a very real and open question—would he actually keep going, and if so, go where? I was out of touch with Jim during these years. Many of us were. Jim faced many demons during those dark years. Once, he told me of a time he was in Hawaii and driving his wheelchair drunk one night, trying to decide whether or not to just steer himself off a cliff. I wouldn't have blamed him, not one bit.

So let's get real about what he was up against:

No movement from the waist down.

No control of his bowels or bladder.

No sexual function.

Limited movement of his arms and hands (which was a big surprise to the doctors).

Chronic pain and fatigue.

The necessity of continual and on-going medical care.

No freedom of movement.

Continual infections and treatment for infections.

Even if I could have seen him during those years, I doubt I would have had the courage to. I felt the same fear many of us felt when thinking of going to see Jim after that second accident: the fear of not knowing what to say to him, of wanting to apologize for the world, for life. The fear, deep down, of facing the great unavoidable truth Jim MacLaren put in front of us by his very existence: that really terrible, ghastly stuff happens to good and beautiful people for no apparent rhyme or reason. It can happen to any one of us, or to people we love, at any time. That's the truth which Jim made clear, and I avoided it by avoiding him.

But Jim was full of surprises. I am not my body, he said. This made all the more poignant since what a glorious body he had.

I saw Jim for the first time after the second accident in the late nineties or early oughts in Boulder, Colorado, where my Mom lives and where Jim had moved. I was terrified. But here's what I remember. I remember the distinct sense that Jim knew this re-connection was

17

harder for me than it was for him and that he was trying to make it easier for me. We spent an hour or two together, and after the first ten minutes I felt like I was back with that guy I went to Florida with, fifteen year earlier. I was experiencing the eternal and essential Jimness of Jim again. I was experiencing his spirit, which I fell in love with in 1982, which lasts forever and which no tragedy could ever quell. I am not my body, he showed me, I am something mysterious and unnameable.

We thought Jim had become the biggest star possible with the triathlons and all. But—surprise! In the beginning of this century, Jim co-founded the Challenged Athletes Foundation and began a very successful motivational speaking business, assisted by his sister Jen. And what a speaker he was. Here's another excerpt:

> I can still say, as objectively as possible, that I wouldn't trade what happened to me. Having to admit to my own dependency and vulnerability—hiring caregivers, having to travel with somebody, needing someone to help me take care of my business life—these were all decisions that actually made me more powerful. Why? It finally dawned on me that acknowledging your wounds and vulnerabilities, and becoming more conscious and knowledgeable about yourself, actually makes you a stronger person. I've learned how to let people in who really love me, and say, "I'm hurting and I'm human and I need some help." If I can look at my life truthfully and accept everything that's happened to me, then I can believe that I'm always going to be okay.

Over the next eight years, Jim, in his wheelchair, became something of a celebrity, and the myth entered its fourth act. The pinnacle of this time in his life was certainly his being named, along with Emmanuel Ofosu Yeboah, the ESPN Arthur Ashe Courage Award winner for

2005. The story of that award, and Jim's remarkable relationship with this inspiring young man from Ghana, is well documented. Search "Jim MacLaren" on YouTube. You won't be disappointed.

If the triathlon years were marked by an obsessive self-focus for Jim, then the wheelchair years were marked by an equally obsessive outward focus. During the last ten years of his life, Jim made it his mission to reach people who needed help, to inspire people who needed inspiration, and to love virtually everyone. Those dark years of the late nineties were the crucible in which Jim made the decision to live. And once having made that decision, he had to live the only way he knew how—big. Full of surprises. Larger than life. And exuding love and good humor.

Sometimes God picks one of us and makes an example out of them. You don't have to believe this. But I do. I believe that God made an example out Jim MacLaren. And it's not an Old Testament example. It's not, "Behold my power and my wrath." No. It's look at what you human beings are really made of, really capable of. Watch, as I take away Jim's leg. See? He becomes a triathlete. You can be like that. Watch, as I take away just about everything else. See? He becomes more loving, smart, open, and generous than he has ever been before. You can be like that. You can, but without losing everything. I draw your attention to Jim MacLaren, God says. I make him a myth. Look, listen and learn.

In my worst moments, I ask myself: can I be like Jim?

The fifth act of Jim's life confirms that the play was indeed a tragedy. Through a series of economic collapses Jim lost nearly all his financial resources, and in 2009 he ended up alone in an assisted living facility in California. I had no idea about any of this. Not many of his friends did, so fast and so drastic was his downfall. But his sister did, and after going to see him, Jennifer rallied Jim's friends to his side, and many people—many people sitting here today—contributed money and other resources to get Jim across the country and into a subsidized apartment in Akron, Pennsylvania, so that he could be near Jen and her family, and they could monitor his care. From late 2009 through early 2010, Jen, Jim and his doctors worked on stabilizing his health, which had become a nearly constant battle with virulent infections, infections which were becoming more and more resistant to the antibiotics used to fight them.

This is how Jim came back into my life. Jim's apartment was a little over an hour's drive from my house, and so when Jen gave me the word that Jim was strong enough to have visitors, I began to see Jim again on a regular basis. From last March through August, I drove out to see Jim once every one or two weeks, just to sit at his bedside, drink his coffee, and shoot the shit.

While he made valiant efforts to get back in his chair, Jim was essentially bedridden at the end of his life. I saw my role as simply a companion, a listener, a joker. Someone just to help Jim feel like he was still a real person, with real connections with the world and to his own past. I tried to nudge Jim into visions of what the next act might look like. Back into theater maybe? Jim spoke to me recently of wanting to turn his motivational speeches into a fully theatrical one-man play, weaving in stories from the myths loved, indeed, that he was an expert on. He shocked me and my friend Pearce when we dropped by to visit in June, by reciting a famous passage from another David Mamet play, a notoriously vulgar diatribe which Jim snapped off to our amazement and to great comic effect. He was sharp, spot-on, focused, full of humor and grace, even as he lay in what he probably assumed was his deathbed. Full of surprises—right up to the end.

In mid-August, I went with my family on a two-week road trip. My eleven-year-old son had been hearing me talk about Jim all summer and asked me when he was going to meet him. "When we get back," I told him. Monday the 30th of August, I called Jim and left a message to say we were home and that I wanted to bring Griffen with me to see him that Thursday. Jim died early the next morning, finally succumbing to the infections he had fought so long and so hard. Finally slipping into the peace he deserved. Finally released.

Some have wondered aloud to me—did he take his own life? Let me say emphatically that he did not. Jim had looked suicide in the face long before and had made up his mind. He chose life, because he knew it was a gift and he wanted to wring every last drop of magic from it.

"For me, the journey has always been about going deeper and becoming more of a human being," Jim MacLaren said. Jim continues: "And, you know what, just once in a while being okay with the fact that it's fricking hard. It's just hard, and it's not fair. And when I say that, I'm saying that for everybody in the world. Somehow we were brought up to believe that life is fair, and that if we're good, then it's all going to always be good. But stuff happens. Is it fair what's happened to me? No, of course not. So what? I still have to get up in

21

the morning. It's not about overcoming adversity, it's about living with adversity."

Jim MacLaren is my hero. Not because he went to Yale College and the Yale School of Drama. Not because he's in the Triathlon Hall of Fame. Not even because he won the Arthur Ashe Courage Award. No. Jim's my hero, because last March, as I left his room, he raised up his wounded arms and beckoned me to come closer. I did, and he held me close to him on his bed and he kissed me, again, and said, "I love you, bro." Jim told me he loved me, every time we saw each other. And I said it back. And we both meant it.

How? How, after everything?

Because, Benny, I am not my body.

Thank you for being here.

3 FROM *SIXTY SECONDS:*
ONE MOMENT CHANGES EVERYTHING
by Phil Bolsta

MacLaren, a motivational speaker and author, has triumphed over two horrific accidents that would have destroyed a lesser man. At twenty-two, he was a Yale All-American athlete and aspiring actor when his motorcycle was broadsided by a New York City bus. Dead on arrival, he woke up after an eight-day coma to find his left leg amputated below the knee. Inspired by a book about triathlons, he became the fastest one-legged endurance athlete on the planet, routinely finishing ahead of most able-bodied athletes. Eight years later, a van plowed into him during a race, rendering him a quadriplegic. Since then, MacLaren has created the Choose Living Foundation, earned two master's degrees, and is working towards his Ph.D. in Mythology and Depth Psychology. The following is Jim's story, in his own words.

I was having an early morning cup of coffee on Saturday, June 5, 1993, the day before a major triathlon in Mission Viejo, California. I was sitting on my girlfriend's porch in Boulder, Colorado, reflecting on a pretty heady book I was reading, *The Secret Doctrine* by H.P. Blavatsky. Although I was up on a porch, covered by trees, I could hear families walking to breakfast with their children on the street below. It was such a beautiful, pristine summer day. I was gazing at the trees and the huge rock faces in the distance and looking back over the eight years since I had lost my leg. I remember thinking, *Wow, I've really reinvented myself. I'm a professional triathlete. ESPN is following me in the race tomorrow, and I'm traveling around the world racing and doing motivational talks. And it hit me. I thought, Wow, I'm back in it. I'm back in life.*

Out of nowhere, I started crying. My girlfriend and training partner came out on the porch with a cup of coffee, saw me crying, and asked, "What's the matter?" I smiled through tears and said, "Nothing is the matter. I'm crying because I'm happy. Something amazing is about to happen to me. I can just feel it."

Fast forward eighteen hours later. I wake up early, get to the race and again, I'm feeling wonderful because I'm being announced along with the top pros. The race starts. I finish the mile swim and hop on my bike. A couple miles into the bike ride on a closed course, I'm stretched out on my aerodynamic handlebars, just flying. I assumed the people watching were applauding—until I realized they were screaming. I look over to my left, and coming right at me is the grill of a black van. I learned later that a traffic marshal had misjudged my speed approaching the intersection and had directed the van to cross the street.

Life in these moments really slows down. I remember thinking, *Okay, if I pedal one click faster, I can beat this guy across the intersection.* The last thing I remember hearing is people screaming and the driver hitting his accelerator instead of his brakes. He struck my back wheel, I was thrown from my bike, flew headfirst into a signpost, and broke my neck.

None of that I remember. I woke up in the ambulance, still in race mode, feeling the adrenaline. I was in the same state of mind I had been in eight years earlier. When I first woke up after getting hit by that bus and saw that my left leg was missing, I thought, *Oh, okay, cool, your left leg's gone.* And I went back to sleep. When I woke up the day after that, that's when my ego and brain started freaking out.

So when I came to in the ambulance, I knew right away that my legs didn't work. But I remember thinking, *Oh, maybe I'm just a paraplegic. Maybe I'll be able to wheelchair race. And I could go beat Jim Knaub* (who held all the wheelchair marathon records). Then I blacked out again.

The next thing I know, I'm in the hospital, outside the OR. A doctor is holding my hand. He tells me straight, "Look, you're a C5-C6 quad, which means that you broke your neck right up around your ears, and you're never going to move or feel again from the chest down for the rest of your life." At that moment, there was some aspect of me that felt that if he never let go of my hand, that I'd be okay. But, of course, he had to let go because they wheeled me into the OR. That was the start of multiple surgeries and months of being in the ICU. Basically, the inferno had begun. It was hell. When a buddy from Yale came to see me, I rolled over, looked at him and said, "I don't know if I can do this again." Because I didn't.

As I look back—it's been fourteen years now—there aren't a lot of days where I feel great physically. There are a lot of things that I've lost—my fiancée, much of my independence, the use of my left shoulder due to a failed rotator cuff surgery. But that's life. I had a choice: I could lose myself to my body or learn to live beyond it. I found my strength by saying and believing that I am not my body. I am a man. I am alive, as alive as anybody who's jamming a basketball or scoring a touchdown or hugging their child.

Even though both accidents were devastating at the time, I now view them as gifts and not tragedies. Granted, it might have been easier to say that eighteen months ago, because the last year and a half has been literally miserable. During trips to the hospital, I picked up mono, Chronic Fatigue Syndrome, and an antibiotic-resistant bacteria, which is a real trip. So I've been spending most every day getting up, going to the bathroom, and going back to bed. But even through those tough times, magic happens.

Even though I'm now considered an "incomplete quad" because I have full sensation and movement to varying degrees, I'm still in chronic pain 24/7. Mornings are the worst—I wake up and feel like wet cement plugged into the wall. If I were going to think, *Okay, the rest of my day is going to go exactly how I feel right now*, I'd never get up. But that's not what I do. I start moving my legs a little bit, and my bed becomes an exercise mat. And when I'm up in my chair and sitting on the porch, it's a hundred times better than the way I felt when I woke up.

I've learned to engage life on whatever level I can, whether it's doing sit-ups in bed or calling friends during the three or four hours it takes for me to get ready in the morning. I've made a ritual out of it. Engaging life, feeling that life force surge through me, helps me recapture the sort of feeling I had in Boulder the day before that big race that something amazing was going to happen to me. Well, something amazing did happen. Maybe not the way Merriam-Webster defines it, but yeah, something pretty amazing happened to me.

Granted, some days are harder than others. I was on an NPR radio show with my friend Bob Kerrey, the former U.S. senator from Nebraska who's missing a leg. The radio host asked Bob if he considers the loss of his leg a gift, and Bob said, "Yeah, I believe it's a gift, but some mornings it's a gift I'd like to wake up without." I feel the same way. There are times I don't like the way my life went, but that doesn't mean that I'm not in love with life.

So, yeah, even though the last eighteen months have been hell, I can still say, as objectively as possible, that I wouldn't trade what happened to me. Having to admit to my own dependency and vulnerability actually made me more powerful. Why? It dawned on me that acknowledging your wounds and vulnerabilities, and becoming more conscious and knowledgeable about yourself, actually makes you a stronger person. I've learned how to let people in who really love me, and say, "I'm hurting and I'm human and I need some help." If I can look at my life truthfully and accept everything that's happened to me, then I can believe that I'm always going to be okay. What I believe in obviously works, and it's in my soul, because otherwise I would've tried to step over my balcony.

People often tell me things like, "You have such a strong will" or "You have such an amazing attitude," but there's just never been a thought in me about, *Boy, if I was just the way I used to be, I wouldn't be going through all this BS. It's always been, Okay, here's a new challenge; let me figure it out, let me face it.* For me, the journey has always been about going deeper and becoming more of a human being. And, you know what, just once in a while being okay with the fact that it's fricking hard. It's just hard, and it's not fair. And when I say that, I'm saying that for everybody in the world. Somehow we were brought up to believe that life is fair, and that if we're good, then it's all going to always be good. But stuff happens. Is it fair what's happened to me? No, of course not. So what? I still have to get up in the morning. It's not about overcoming adversity, it's about living with adversity.

There's a myth from Finland that embracing depth psychology, or probing your own depths, is like setting out across a thousand-mile tundra by yourself. It's not easy. It doesn't always mean that you get the girl or that you get to walk, but maybe it gives you peace.

4 TRIBUTES TO JIM

Clothilde Ewing: Former senior associate producer, *Oprah Winfrey Show*

Clothilde Ewing says Jim MacLaren is the guest she'll never forget.

He told me that he saw both accidents as a gift because, he said, it wasn't until that second accident that he realized what was really important in life. Meeting Jim taught me why it's important to be positive, and he also taught me that anything is possible.

Hillary Wing-Richards: Jim MacLaren's mom

To my son Jim,

We began our life together on April 13, 1963. Not only was I young but also not fully aware what it meant to be a mother. All I knew was that I was thrilled and excited to meet you. You came into the world a big boy and gave me an immediate feeling of deep and enduring love every time I looked at you.

Years went by and you never ceased to amaze me. Everyone talks of your academic achievements and athletic abilities, but I am speaking of your ability to love and be so full of energy and interest in the world. I recall the business trips you went on with Grandpa. After one of those trips, when you were only 8 years old, he told me, "That boy is going to be something special one day."

You were already special to me, Jim. Now each day I think of you and hope you feel the love I have and always have had for you. How proud I am to speak of you to friends and students who then go to a computer to look up your story. But most important—you are my son, and for that I will always be so grateful.

Love you, Jim.

Sean O'Malley: Creator, Cardio Coach Guided Workouts

Words of love for a grieving sister from a man who never really knew his true strength but lent it to so many in his short lifetime.

The "thing" about your brother is that he has left his energy all over this planet. I don't think I ever told you this. Shortly after Jim passed away, I came home from teaching a class one night and a dove was sitting on the railing directly in front of my parent's kitchen window. I took a picture every 5 feet with the concern it was going to fly away. It let me get within a few feet. My parents said they have never seen a bird rest on the railing in the 5 years they lived there.

I looked up the symbology, and according to some, and depending on what you believe, it means a spirit was set free to heaven. The next night, a very large dragonfly was resting in the light under my door when I came home. I lost a lot of my beliefs over the last few years, and I'm still not sure how to take it but at least it is a comforting thought.

You may know that I always believed I was connected to Jim in an unusual way. It may have been for an overall good, but the connection often felt more like a trapped feeling—as though I was trapped with Jim. When I saw that dove fly away that night, it was what I needed to see.

Missing Jim is something that will probably never go away, and I hope it doesn't. But you have to combine those thoughts with knowing how many lives he not only changed but improved as well. You have to remember that, Jennifer. It makes missing him a little less sharp, I would have to believe. I think of the love you have for him and it always reminds me of the love my sister has always had for me. You are both very special people in that way. You are our protectors.

I have to tell you this one last thing, though I may have told you before. When Karal first introduced me to Jim in 2005, I started doing some research and came across a very old forum thread. You had posted a "missing" thread to find your brother. You found him and you never let go—even when he did his damnedest to pull away. You hung on like a pit bull. I don't know if in life we ever do everything possible to hold on to a situation. I think there is always just a little bit more that can be done. But you far exceeded the human threshold for keeping Jim with us for much longer than he would have made it without you.

To a world who has given us loving sisters!

Love, Sean

Doug Wright: Pulitzer Prize-winning writer, friend, Yale roommate

A dozen snapshots of Jimmy Mac

When someone achieves mythic stature in life, like Jim MacLaren, it grows difficult to capture them in words; they become a compendium of achievements, the sum total of challenges overcome, records set, races won, speeches given, and awards bestowed. By the end of his too-short life, Jim had amassed a heady array of such triumphs, and he came by them all with integrity, worth, and at times almost inconceivable sacrifice.

But I would be loath to see his impressive résumé slowly erase the man beneath; I hope that with the passage of time, I'll still remember the more ephemeral aspects of a life as richly and fully lived as his. I never want to lose sight of Jim's wicked sense of humor, his keen intellect, and his seemingly boundless compassion. To that end, I'd like to offer twelve fleeting snapshots of the man I recall. Most of them date from college, when we were roommates together at Yale in the early 1980's. But all of them, I think, illuminate core aspects of Jim's nature, and most of them still make me smile. Some (I freely admit) border on hagiography. If others reveal (in often comic ways) some of Jim's foibles as well, it's only because I believe that the most loving tribute is also the most accurate one.

#1

It's the spring of 1984, and Jim Maclaren approaches me in our university dining hall. Everyone on campus recognizes him by his gargantuan frame; he's one of the football team's most valued players.

I know him in a different context: as a fellow student in our junior year acting class, where he tackles scenes from George Bernard Shaw and David Mamet with equal dexterity. I flatter myself that I've had a privileged glimpse into his sensitive side.

"Hey," he tells me with a sly smile, "They just posted our rankings for room picks next year. You and I got top of the list."

"Cool," I tell him, trying to maintain my own equilibrium in the face of his overwhelming presence. I am a tightly wound, closeted gay student in the Theater Studies Department; he is the very definition of Big Man on Campus. We make a strange pair, lingering together by the salad bar.

"Separately, we could each vie for one of the premium single rooms," he reasons, "but together, if we unite forces, we could get the best freaking double in all of Pierson College."

I gulp. Should I leave my stalwart chums behind, the two Daves who've been my roommates for three solid years, and shack up with a veritable stranger, one who intimidates me at that?

"Yeah," I say. "That'd be great."

#2

Jim has just been cast as the mentally infirm but lovable Lenny in a student production of John Steinbeck's landmark drama *Of Mice and Men*. As a freshman, he's thrilled to get such a plum role, but he's also harboring doubts.

Like Lenny, Jim comes from humble stock; he's paved his own way through boarding school and college. Jim's also a forbidding physical presence, at over 6 feet 4 inches tall and 275 pounds. But beyond these similarities, Jim worries about the possible stigma of portraying someone that might uncharitably be referred to as "retarded." Given his prowess on the field and his mammoth stature, Jim worries that he's the victim of unflattering stereotypes; the curse of the "dumb jock." He doesn't want to buttress that perception in the roles he chooses to play. In his heart, Jim is bedeviled by thoughts that he isn't smart enough to be at Yale, and that he's under increased scrutiny to prove his intellectual worth. (Anyone who's sat in class with Jim and heard him speak knows this is flagrantly preposterous; but we all have insecurities the larger, wiser world deems absurd.)

Ultimately, Jim accepts the role and delivers a heart wrenching, nuanced, even profound performance.

#3

Jim and I are decorating our senior year suite. He provides a killer stereo and slick new contraption called an "answering machine." We have (drum roll, please) a private bath, a rarity in college housing. I decide to spruce it up with black and white photos of sultry, half-naked male models I find in some old issue of *Interview* magazine. When Jim sees my handiwork for the first time, he's a bit flummoxed. After a long pause (I'm on tenterhooks), he says, "It's weird, but it's hip."

Almost daily, one of Jim's athletic friends will come pounding on our door to woo him out for a beer or a courtyard game of scrimmage. When I answer the door—in my zoot suit trousers and my artsy, ruffled scarf—our visitor's face slackens and he mutters under his breath, "I must have the wrong room. I'm looking for Jimmy Mac?"

Similarly, when a member of my comparatively Bohemian tribe

arrives, smoking clove cigarettes and speaking with the sort of affected British accent so beloved by acting students at Ivy League campuses, he or she is stunned when a strapping Jim swings open the door to the sound of Springsteen wailing on his powerhouse sound system. "Yeah?" he asks. "Sorry," my classmate mutters, "my mistake. I'm looking for Doug?"

Secretly, when the door is closed, we both howl with glee at our "odd couple" status. It's a source of constant amusement between us.

#4

It's lunchtime, and a table full of young college women are picking at their salads. They don't know that I'm within earshot. I'm friendly with most of them, and I know them to be savagely articulate, ferociously bright, and admirably ambitious. But today, effervescing about Jim, they've been reduced to, well, giddy girls.

"He's just so *gi*-normous," one sighs. "Can you imagine kissing him? You'd have to scale him first, like he were some mountain!"

"I know!" squeals another. "I'd just like to climb all over him, like an ant on a hill."

"And his smile!" trills another. "Can you *believe* that smile?"

Together, they pledge that if given the chance, they'd all give themselves over to Jim for a night of reckless abandon. In fact, they seem to be making it part of a collegiate bucket list.

A few weeks later, I can't resist. I ask Jim if the scheduled bacchanalia ever came to fruition.

"Come on, Doug," he grins. "You know I don't kiss and tell."

Traditionally, Yale has been light on Greek life, but offers instead "senior societies"; rarified, Old World clubhouses where chosen students congregate to bond together in an atmosphere of camaraderie and stiff-backed tradition.

Jim and I were both members of the same club. Ours featured an array of stellar young men: captains of the football, lacrosse, hockey, swimming, and baseball teams; the student chair of the African-American Studies Center; the leading debater and the class president. I was the token *artiste,* known for the precocious plays and performances I contributed to the dramatic society.

The group's single-sex status made it a lightning rod for criticism, especially by women. And yet while I agreed with their objections, I'd joined it for that very reason. I'd never been a member of an all-male group; I certainly wasn't proficient enough to join a sports team, and I'd had scant experience "pounding back brewskies" with macho peers. I both feared and craved that kind of experience. My best friends had always been female; at last, I hoped, I'd be one of the guys. I had few bona fide creds as a "bro," but my status as Jimmy Mac's roommate helped boost my otherwise scant credentials.

Unfortunately, that same year, I knew I had to publicly identify as gay. The secret had become overwhelming and toxic; I'd hidden it for years, and it threatened to capsize my mental health and wellbeing. To ready myself, I'd been making regular trips to the free psychiatric services offered through the Medical School. Counseling, I hoped, would ease my path. I'd hedged my bets by stockpiling sleeping pills in our medicine cabinet, in case the world turned on me.

Our club was full of sensitive, even progressive fellows, but they weren't immune to male posturing: tales of late-night sexual conquests, racy jokes, and plenty of anxiety about homosexuality. This unease found its expression in callous remarks and rising suspicions about me. One night, a member of our cadre asked me point-blank if I was a "faggot." I promptly resigned from the organization and fled the premises, distraught.

I'd never spoken to Jim about my inner turmoil, but he'd divined it. He was too empathetic at heart and too skilled a reader of human nature not to; and in fairness, what I perceived as my own irrevocably dark mystery was probably pretty obvious.

After my abrupt departure, an enraged Jim had convened the group in our clubhouse. "He's one of us, and you turn on him that way? When we pledged to support and honor one another?"

For hours, he passionately argued my case. Less than twenty years after Stonewall and thirty years before gay marriage hit the headlines, Jim was speaking up for my inclusion, and not because he was an activist on this particular cause. He spoke because he was simply my friend, and he knew I needed someone in my corner. He was a better advocate for me than I could have been for myself, and the ferocious big brother I so urgently needed in those fragile times.

Some days later, I received a beautiful handwritten note from my brethren, asking me to please reinstate my membership. In it, they apologized for their insensitivity and expressed a sincere desire to learn more about what it meant to be gay in a hostile world. I was more than touched; their missive saved me from my own despair.

Years later, I would laugh, "When I came out of the closet, Jim was there, holding the door open for me."

#6

Jim is unabashedly weeping as he gently lowers the kitten into a cardboard box. We discovered it howling on the eaves of the roof outside our window; in its pink belly, a horrible slash. Seeking solace from the cold, it crawled up into a car engine for warmth. When a hapless driver started the ignition, the damage was done. It climbed to safety, and now it's screeching for its life, or at least respite from the agonizing pain.

Cradling the box in one arm, Jim mounts his motorcycle and goes blaring into the night; he's found a twenty-four-hour veterinarian, and he's determined to give the poor critter the best possible chance for survival. He has no money to pay for feline surgery, but he has credit cards, and he's willing to max them out if that's what it takes.

He comes home bereft, his face pale and his shoulders weak from crying. The animal was past saving; the vet had to put it down. Jim held it as it quietly drifted out of consciousness, gently stroking its fur. When he tells me this, I'm reminded of Steinbeck's Lenny and his beloved rabbits.

A few weeks later, Jim and I sneak a small grey cat into our quarters. We name it Hoover. He's a little hellion. We double over with laughter as we watch him zigzag around the room like a tiny demon, possessed.

#7

Senior year of college and it's my birthday. I've never celebrated on campus before; since I'm a mid-December baby, the date has historically fallen during our scheduled winter break. But this year, school is still in session. Nevertheless, it's finals week, and few people have the time or inclination to kick up their heels.

That night, en route to dinner, Jim suddenly squires me into a private banquet room on campus. He's gathered all our friends. To make the evening especially festive, he's gone to the drugstore and gotten a host of children's birthday supplies; everyone is sporting Mickey Mouse hats, and Pin the Tail on Eeyore is mounted on the wall.

"Twenty-one," he tells me. "Your last night to be a kid." He places his hand on my shoulder and adds wistfully, "Make the most of it."

#8

Jim has just finished his first day as an acting student at the prestigious training program known as Circle in the Square. He's sitting on my floor, beer in hand, his giant feet splayed out haphazardly. But his face is lit from within, like some beatific saint. In tones that vacillate between unfettered enthusiasm and awed reverence, he's describing his morning.

"Our instructor Michael Kahn is this theatrical guru," he tells me. "And the curriculum is unbelievable; we'll do physical work, with elements of Feldenkrais, and vocal work, too, with speech therapists and dialect coaches. We'll learn fencing for classical roles. I may even learn to sing. It's too much, man."

His happy banter is infectious; it carries me along on a bubbly high.

When I look at him, I can't help but wonder if he'll one day bound across a Broadway stage as Petruchio, or light up film screens as some new breed of action hero. It seems more than just likely; it seems inevitable.

#9

I've been summoned in the middle of the night to Bellevue Hospital, where I am told that Jim has been admitted after suffering a life-threatening accident on his motorcycle. Along with his mother and sister, I'm escorted to intensive care. He lies there, unrecognizable, under a labyrinthine web of tubes, his face bruised beyond recognition. I can tell that underneath the sheet lying wanly over his body, one leg is gone.

Months later, I visit Jim at a rehab facility in New Jersey. His face is unblemished, his signature grin intact. He's slimmer than I've ever seen him, giving his face the obvious bone structure of a matinee idol. His brow is furrowed in intense concentration as he takes his first, tentative steps on a new prosthetic limb. It's victory enough; I don't dare posit that one day, he will run. He will swim. He will exceed all rational expectation.

#10

The Toledo Symphony Orchestra is playing, their music floating past on a beguiling breeze. Waiters in tuxedos are passing canapés, and champagne glasses are clinking. Jim is marrying into one of the grand, old high-society families of Ohio and no expense has been spared.

It's a heady trip for a man who used to scrounge for the payments on his beloved motorcycle and was no stranger to short-term loans.

Jim has borne the curse of others like him, strivers who find themselves moving in socio-economic strata far beyond their own: he has an unfettered love of the finer things. Tonight, he is luxuriating in them; white linen tablecloths with matching orchids; Baccarat crystal candlesticks.

Years later, the fantasy will dissolve in the unfortunate reality of divorce. But tonight—infatuated by the promise of a life free of future hardship—Jim has the beguiling expression of a boy on Christmas morning.

"It's good to be King," he whispers to me.

#11

I've heard through the grapevine that Jim is living in New Mexico and has fallen on bleak times. He's divorced, solitary, and fighting the constant threat of infection. His body is in almost constant pain. His financial resources have trickled away, and his ego has taken a correlative nosedive. His *Sports Illustrated* cover is a fast-receding memory, and his appearances on the lecture circuit have ended due to his failing health.

I'm confident that I can buck him up with a farcical anecdote from days gone by: that night we got plastered in the New Haven cemetery and scared ourselves silly, or the time I interrupted an unexpected game of strip poker.

I ring him several times. I press "send" on five or six emails. Jim does not respond. Days go by, and then weeks, and I don't hear from him. I'm disappointed, but I'm not wholly surprised. Our relationship is built on the underlying precept that he is my protector and hero; I'm the tousled, bespectacled kid with the Muppets backpack, and he is my playground bodyguard. It's hard enough for him to lower his guard and ask for help, but to ask me specifically? That's impossible.

#12

After his well-publicized travails and his celebrity status in the sports world, Jim is a coveted guest at our twenty-fifth college reunion. Underneath the big, white tents on verdant lawns, set with tables and bar stations, he is the man everyone wants to welcome. He's one of the few who can make a wheelchair look genuinely stylish; he sits in at an insouciant angle, like he's lounging in a portable lawn chair. The black bands he wears on his hands to better power the wheels resemble chic fashion accessories from some SoHo boutique; his expensive sunglasses are resting on top of his head, among his tousled mane of Clark Kent hair. Our class boasts senators, Hollywood actors, film producers, and public policy wonks, but they're jostling for their moment with Jimmy Mac.

But Jim's attention is elsewhere. My goddaughter, an adorable creature with doe-like eyes and the innocence to match, is standing next to him. They are in rapt conversation. Too young to know better, Molly is peppering him with blunt questions: "What happened to you? How come you only have one leg? Is the other one plastic?" Jim is charmed by her directness; he answers each query with patience, even appreciation for her curiosity.

Finally, he asks, "So have you ever ridden one of these babies?" A bit cowed, Molly shakes her head "no." Jim reaches for her, and draws her onto his lap.

"Hold on," he admonishes, and they're off. Soon, everyone is watching them careen across the grass, their hair rising in the wind, Molly's hands outstretched and her face beaming. It's a remarkable sight, this death-defying athlete taking a diminutive blonde girl on the ride of her life.

As the wheels churn beneath her, Molly is learning lessons that neither her parents nor I could ever teach.

She is learning that even the cruelest obstacles can be overcome; that a terrible accident can be transformed from tragedy to liberation; that even though you're in a wheelchair, you can still take glorious flight.

Bill Fink: Friend

Jim was my client prior to being my good friend, though the friendship followed immediately. Jim was that kind of person. You became his friend immediately regardless of the situation.

I met Jim through a realtor by the name of Bob Lasswell (who also became a great friend to Jim, no surprise there, and to me). Bob told me that he had a client who was buying a condo in downtown San Diego and wondered if I could put together the loan. He also told me that his client had an amazing story to tell and that he was a quadriplegic. To be honest, at the time the sound of the word "quadriplegic" made me a bit uncomfortable. I had never known a quadriplegic before. I fretted about how I should act around Jim if I ever met him in person.

Most of my early dealings with Jim were over the phone. Even over the phone, I could tell that Jim was an incredible human being. He spoke with a presence. I knew that he was a motivational speaker; even over the phone he motivated people. Talking to Jim made you instantly feel better about being alive. To Jim, the world was out there to be discovered, studied, and cherished. And man was he smart.

One day when Jim needed to sign some mortgage papers, I asked him if I should just overnight the papers for him to sign, but he told me that he would be in the area and would like to stop by. I wondered how this was even possible. Wasn't he a quadriplegic? How would he get to my office? I just figured that he had a driver. It seemed like a lot of trouble so I asked him again if I could just get him the papers. He wouldn't have it. A short time later that day, Jim called me from his cell phone and told me he was in the parking lot. I grabbed the papers and went outside to meet Jim and his driver. Only thing was, there was no driver. Instead, there sat Jim in the driver's seat of his van, a huge smile on his face, and holding a cigarette no less. What kind of quadriplegic *was* this?

After the loan closed and Jim and I talked more and more about his business and finance, Jim asked me to become his financial advisor. I then began going over to Jim's condo 2–3 times a week to open his mail, pay his bills, update his financials, go over his budget, and mainly chew the bull. We would also meet at the Westfield UTC Mall outdoor food court in La Jolla not far from my condo at the time. Jim would sip his coffee and I would drink my iced green tea. Jim loved to people watch and boy could he talk. And Jim being who he was, he had no fears whatsoever about talking to anyone, anytime, about anything. He and I would talk about sports, politics, women, money, music, movies, and food. What we didn't talk about was Jim's ailments. He wouldn't have it. Any early uneasiness I may have had about "Jim, the quadriplegic" dissipated quickly. All I began seeing was "Jim, the person." I knew that he had to overcome an incredible amount of suffering to get to where he was, but I didn't know Jim's story for another year. He never told me directly. If he needed help with something, he asked. But most of the time he just wanted to be as independent as possible. Being so full of life, Jim liked to spend money. He made quite a living as a motivational speaker back in those days before the great recession crushed us all, but he simply wasn't a saver. Any little arguments Jim and I ever had were about me wanting Jim to save more. And Jim could be quite the businessman as well. When it came to his career and his Choose Living Foundation, another side of Jim came out: the take-no-shit side.

In July 2005, Jim told me that he was going to receive the Arthur Ashe Courage Award at the ESPYS, that Oprah of all people was going to present it to him, and that he had a ticket for me to go. "I'd be honored," I responded. "And holy crap Jim, that is incredible." He was so amped up about the award, as he should have been. The day before the ESPYS, Jim once again stopped by my office to sign some paperwork on a second downtown San Diego condo purchase that started out as a rental property but eventually became his office. I was working on some other deals at the time and was on the phone while Jim signed the papers. After Jim was finished signing, I watched out of the corner of my eye as Jim proceeded to stand up out of his wheelchair with some great difficulty. He fought through it until he was finally standing. I, however, was too busy on the phone to even acknowledge it.

Here's a guy who at some point was told that he would never move a muscle, and he's standing up behind my desk. Thousands of hours of sacrifice, pain, and incredibly hard work culminate in one medical miracle moment of brilliance—and I ignore it.

If anything, I was mildly annoyed about not being able to get behind my desk to grab a pen to take some notes about the call I was on. I didn't think much of it until the next day.

I arrived at the ESPYS, picked up my ticket, and got to my seat. I was solo and was excited to be there in support of Jim. The show went on for quite some time and then suddenly, there was Jim's face on the big screen. And for the first time I heard Jim's story . . . both in Oprah's words and Jim's. The early football success, Yale, a promising career in acting, the motorcycle ride down Tenth Avenue in New York City . . . then devastation, the city bus, the coma, the struggles, the rehab, the rise as an Ironman champion . . . then yet even more devastation, the black van, the paralysis. . . . It was all too much.

I sobbed, tears streaming down my face, along with most of the audience. They cried mostly because they felt bad for Jim (though the last thing Jim would ever want is for someone to feel bad for him). I sobbed because I couldn't help feeling bad for Jim, but mostly because I realized what standing up in my office must have meant to him— something that, as an able-bodied person, I took for granted every day. I vowed to apologize to Jim and to never again let the phone get in the way of appreciating life's miracles.

My heart heavy with guilt, I apologized profusely to Jim a few days later, again with tears in my eyes. However, he quickly waved me off and told me I was being silly. "You never have to apologize to me for anything buddy," he told me. And that is how I choose to remember Jim, because Jim didn't stand up in my office that day for my benefit. He stood up for himself.

Mickey: Yale University friend

I have a lot of Jimmy Mac stories, but my favorite is this:

The Yale lacrosse team used to practice in a sump-like area, where rain run-off tended to settle. The area didn't drain well at all. Early spring practices were more akin to a bunch of guys mud-wrestling with helmets and clubs.

At one practice, I had the ball and went to the cage. Each step was like moving through wet cement. Jimmy not only was the biggest guy on the team, he was also the fastest. When he hit you, your brain kind of rattled around inside your skull. He hit me so hard that day that I came out of my cleats, which remained implanted in the mud. The next thing I saw, after I opened my eyes flat on my back, was Jimmy handing me my cleats and saying, "You forgot to take these . . . . "

Mark Foster: Vermont Academy '83

I was a sophomore when Jim was a senior. He was that guy that you looked up to, and a true leader.

He came on stage one morning meeting in the fall and announced that the football team was short players. I answered his call and tried out. While only making it to JV, it was still an experience I am grateful for.

I followed Jim over the years, and he was one of the reasons I got into triathlons twenty-something years ago. It was his never-give-up attitude that I will continue to embrace. I am a better person for having been a schoolmate and a part of a very special time and place in Vermont. I am honored to have served and supported him in his CAF mission. I will always remember "MACKER!" as he was known on the fields of Vermont.

He will be greatly missed but lives strong in those of us that were fortunate enough to have crossed paths.

Julie Broderick: Friend

When I was asked to write a small tribute for Jim, my first thought was how humbled I was and what a beautiful gift it was to be entrusted with such an important task. My next thought was how in the world could I ever begin to express in words the impact Jim had on my life and how knowing him changed my life in ways I never thought possible.

My connection with Jim began many years ago when I reached out to him after hearing his story. I remember thinking, *this man is the most beautiful soul I have ever known.* There was an instant connection, and we were simply meant to be in each other's lives. Our conversations were deep, and he always made me feel as though I was the most special person on the planet.

Although Jim had many, many challenges in his life, he never once thought that anyone else's challenges were any less than his own—just one of the many things I loved about Jim. We developed such a close bond, friendship, and love over the years and with his guidance, support, and encouragement, I started to run. I completed my first marathon this year and Jim was with me all the way.

Jim is never far from my thoughts and I will carry him in my heart always. My Choose Living bracelet is my most prized running possession, and I wear it each and every time I run. It keeps me focused and gives me strength.

I have also, because of Jim, developed a beautiful friendship with his sister Jennifer. She has been such a blessing to me. I really could go on and on (and on) about Jim and what a bright light he was in my life, but I will end with my favorite quote from Jim, as this is how I try to live my life:

Do you love and are you loved?

Now THAT is an accomplishment. I love you Jim.

Karal Gregory: Family friend

The first time I heard of Jim MacLaren, I was working for his brother as a personal trainer in L.A. I had an intuition that he and my friend, Cardio Coach workout creator Sean O'Malley, would hit it off. So I sent Sean, back in Virginia, Jim's information.

They began an email correspondence with Sean explaining who he was, and how he'd connected, and Jim, in his first reply to Sean, tells him that even though he's not met me, if I'm working for his family, then I'm family, and he'll look after me like he was my big brother. Now mind you, Jim's in San Diego and I'm in Los Angeles, and we've never even met, but that loyalty, that reaching out to his fellow human, was exactly who Jim was at his core.

That was in 2005, and it was another two years before Sean and I would meet Jim in person to interview him for the Press Play workout. And it wasn't until 10 years after that—in the fall of 2017—that I met, in person, Jim's sister, Jennifer. But our friendship had been strong and sustaining through emails and calls and then, Facebook (finally, I knew what she looked like!) and, honestly, likely through lifetimes before now.

Jim and his family have become my family, too, in many ways. Jim made a promise to keep an eye on me and gave me peace of mind in a strange place and time. And with Sean, we created something beautiful and lasting and life-changing for people the world over. Working with Jennifer on this book, bringing Jim's legacy back to life, continuing the work he began as a motivational speaker, is my way of paying it forward so his story can continue to motivate and inspire us all through our most challenging and toughest times.

5 WORDS FROM A SISTER
by Jennifer Hippensteel

Introduction

My brother Jim. A legend, an inspiration, a motivator, a friend, a sibling, a man.

A man who believed that being alive was a good thing, no matter what the circumstance. A man who lived through two life-threatening accidents and, although he lost his left leg and ended up a partial quadriplegic, still loved life and went on to do great things. And in between, he fought the good fight. He fought his demons, embraced his fears, lived his passions, and at times, fought to stay alive.

Jim was my best friend, my client, my mentor, my frustration, my love. His life intersected with mine and never parted until he passed, and still I feel the pull to continue to share his message, his spirit, and his love.

You can't go from being engulfed in someone's life to suddenly nothing with that person—you just can't do that and survive. I tried and was unsuccessful. When Jim passed, my life had a huge empty hole in it. I had my family, my husband, and my life, yet it was no longer complete. I started to feel depressed, which I hid well. I continued to work to care for my family and to function, but it was on a level that I've never experienced before. At night, I would hide out in the bathroom and cry and cry until I couldn't catch my breath, telling the empty space that I couldn't do this, that I needed Jim back. No one listened, no one heard, and my sadness deepened. I was filled with loneliness—so weird, since I was surrounded by people that love me and that I love in return. But nothing stopped the loneliness or the feeling that this life was meant to be this empty. I do not make a good depressed person: I am a doer, a helper, a person who gets things done because I can't stand them just sitting on a "to do" list.

I can't stand wallowing, but suddenly I'm getting very good at it. I know that my brother would not be happy with this new side of me. He counted on me to make things happen for him: to negotiate and close his deals, to get him the best transportation and hotels for his needs, to run interference on those occasions when he couldn't handle talking to people, to take care of him physically when he called for help. This new sister, the one who sometimes just can't focus on anything, would have driven him crazy, would have frustrated him to no end.

The challenge for me is how to change it. Here I am, lost and wandering aimlessly. No direction or light in sight. I can barely look at his pictures hanging around my home and office. I can't listen to or watch his videos. I try to write his story and I hit wall after wall. I'm unable to climb out of this hole I find myself in, but I know I must. If my brother taught me anything, it was how to persevere. I cannot let him down, this man who protected me as much as I protected him over a lifetime of struggles and pain.

Jim was a pioneer. He paved the way in all of his passions. He wanted to be there first, to draw the line, to make a name for himself. To Jim, success meant being known, appreciated, and needed. And he was all of these things in his short life. He did everything full force, and it was both his strength and his weakness. He traveled at the speed of light and excelled in everything he tried. School, sports, acting, speaking, writing—you name it and Jim could master it. He would try, and learn, and discover until he made it so, to his own demise at times.

Everything he did became an addiction. Even when he loved, his light would burn so bright it would overpower the average person. But when things got too close or too complicated, Jim would pull back, leaving in his wake feelings of complete loss and devastation. He gave so much so quickly, but once someone came to need him, he was gone. Moving on to the next spirit in need and in the process protecting himself from getting too close.

I am, without a doubt, the longest female relationship my brother ever had. I'm the one he never closed out for long, because I didn't let him. You see, I needed him as much as he needed me. We talked about everything, and I mean *everything*. We discussed it all, from philosophy and religion to mythology and sex. In the last few weeks of his life we started reading *Many Lives, Many Masters* by Dr. Brian L. Weiss. We were so intrigued with Dr. Weiss's writings and research, and our goal was to read the books and discuss them at length. Overwhelmed with family and work and Jim's care, I kept putting it off, and I regret so much that we never got to have our conversation. I have many regrets, most of them about time. Time I spent doing daily tasks instead of spending quality time with him. I did see him almost every day, or call or text, but I wish so much I had sat with him more, and just breathed.

Jim kept his wheelchair by the side of his bed. He felt that if he ever had a fire or emergency he'd need his chair to be safe. It was his security blanket and he held onto it at night while he slept. The morning he passed we found him gripping his chair so tightly that the paramedics had to unclench his fingers and move the chair to get to him. It was as though even in death he still needed his chair. Months later, I donated it to the Lion's Club, but as the truck pulled away, I found I couldn't breathe. I asked my husband through my tears, "What if Jim needs his chair? What if he's angry at me for giving it away?" My husband reassured me that he didn't need it anymore, but I felt like I had somehow given away his lifeline.

Though it served to hold and protect him, that chair by his bed prevented me from giving him hugs or holding his hands. It was electric, heavy, and hard to move so I would reach around it, or climb on the bed around all his stuff—his computer, his drink tray, his TV remotes—and hug him. He would take his hand and touch it to mine, saying, "I love you, sis." My heart would melt and I would give him anything he wanted. His smile could twist me up inside. He would laugh and sing to me; "Sister Christian" was one of his favorites and he would sing until I smiled and laughed. He just always seemed to care enough to listen to me, to really hear me. He "got me."

He could be such a dear at times and others so very stubborn, so much that at times he hurt himself and others. He loved my kids so much; since he never had children of his own and he and I were so close, a special bond was formed with them. He would talk to them about their day and ask them about their likes and dislikes. When he was making good money he would spoil them with cell phones and his old computers, a huge money loss for him but a huge gain for my kids. Old for Jim would be like 6 months, and he was forever upgrading his Apple products. He bought them iPods and paid for their plane tickets so they could accompany me on his business trips. He loved having us around. He trusted us. We loved and trusted him. When he lived on the West Coast and I was here in the East, he would send me special songs through iTunes, or he would make me a card on his computer. His video emails were the best, and I am thankful that I still have some. When he started to get sick, I began saving them out of fear of losing him and not being able to hear his voice and see his smile again. Occasionally I watch them, but it still hurts so very much.

He always wore a pinky ring that I think was a gift in his swag bag at the 2005 ESPY awards. He won the Arthur Ashe Courage Award that year and got many gifts for being there. He never took this ring off, so the day he died I asked my sister-in-law, Penny, to remove it from his finger and place it on me. It was a little big, but I had to make it work.

Lately, I have been working out a lot and losing some much-needed weight. The ring has gotten bigger and bigger on me, but I still refuse to take it off. Many times it has fallen on the floor, or I find it on a desk or in the kitchen. I just don't want to stop wearing it, though the jeweler says it can't be resized. The other night I was making dinner and realized the ring was gone. I panicked and looked everywhere for it, even in the garbage. The ring was nowhere to be found. I went down to my room and just totally lost it. I couldn't catch my breath; I started to get chest pains. I could not be without this ring. I was not ready for that and most likely never will be.

For about two hours I wasn't sure what to do. I finally got stubborn and went back upstairs to look again. I went through the trash once more, and there it was. I began to cry again, this time from relief and from the realization that the ring could have been thrown away and lost to me forever. Yes, I am still a basket case. I am still buried in that hole he left behind. I know I am not making him proud. But I honestly think he gets it. We had a connection like no other; I know we are soul mates. I used to believe soul mates could only be lovers, but I now know that isn't true. We are connected in so many ways, ways that transcend this earth and this life I am living.

I have sold and given away some of Jim's clothes. He was a shopper and bought only the best. When Jim and his friend Emmanuel Ofosu Yeboah co-won their ESPY, Oprah Winfrey presented it to them. If you check out the movie *Emmanuel's Gift* you will understand why. Emmanuel and Jim lived on opposite sides of the world and through the Challenged Athletes Foundation met and teamed up to do some great things. Emmanuel is another human being that is taking LIFE seriously. He is another pioneer making way for changes and good in this world.

Jim wore a special tuxedo that night. The jacket was a silk blend and had a purple satin lapel. It is gorgeous and he looked fabulous in it. He was on cloud nine. He called me the next day and screamed into the phone, "Sis, I'm a ROCK STAR!" He was so elated. It didn't matter that he had wheeled, not walked, onto that stage the night before— today he was 10 feet tall. I still have that jacket and I will until I die. I can't just get rid of something that was a part of such a huge night for my brother. No one else is worthy of wearing it, so it remains on my clothes rack in a suit bag. I know people would argue that Jim doesn't need material things anymore, and I have to agree. I think perhaps it's me that needs it. For now I will hold onto to any thread of Jim that I can. It's really all I have right now.

So I kept the ring and the tuxedo but let go of the wheelchair and most of his clothes. This was the beginning for me—the beginning of learning to live on this earth without Jim's earthly body. The beginning of learning to love the memories and live my new life with all that he taught me.

The Beginning of My Journey

June 1, 2011. After watching a marathon long weekend of *Sex and the City* episodes, I came to understand what I want to be doing—I want to write. I just want to write. Maybe someone will enjoy it, maybe they won't. But it is in me to write.

I thought of all the notebooks I have filled since I was 10 years old. They get written and stored in a dark cupboard, behind closed doors. I always had this hidden fear that when I die my kids will find them and then need therapy after reading them. I can almost hear it now. "I can't believe Mom wrote that stuff!" So this fear of others not liking or approving of my writings has kept them far away from prying eyes.

I was thinking this morning that we are given such an amazing gift when we have children. They are born these incredible, spiritual little humans, fresh from the spirit world and filled with an abundance of information and news of where they came from. What do we do? We take this wonderful, spiritual little human and we start right away to teach them our ways. Good or bad, twisted or otherwise. We tell them how to think, dress, talk, and if we discover a talent in them we teach them how to do it better, make money on it, be successful. All of this we do out of love and out of a fear-based notion that we must help our children be successful in this world or they will NOT be happy.

The kicker to this is that they came to us already happy—already knowing their path and their purpose. And we spent years helping them forget it. The end result: adult children constantly searching for their purpose, wondering why they aren't happy, fulfilled, loved, in love. Successful.

Where had they gone wrong? What can they do to fix it? Should they read self-help books? Go to a seminar? Meditate? Find a church? And whatever they do they had better hurry because the clock is ticking. We all have a shelf life. However, what we don't always know is our expiration date.

Please understand that I am not blaming parents for this downfall. Most parents love their children and want to do everything right for them. There in and of itself lies the problem: we can't TELL them their purpose, and we honestly can't DO the hard work for them. We can only encourage them to live their passions, to do the things that fill them with joy. To love those that their hearts are attracted to. To fill them with the desire to get to know themselves well enough to know what makes them happy. To know in their hearts that if they follow their passions and do the work that fills them with joy they will BE successful. No matter what it pays or how many material things they possess.

When I lost my big brother in August of 2010, my world came crashing down around me. For years I was his protector, his business partner, his friend, and his confidant. For years he was my protector, my friend, my confidant. Suddenly, he was gone. His presence had consumed my life for so very long that I was lost, adrift on some raft in the ocean, unable to see dry land. I went through all the stages of grief. Quite honestly I think I am still in them and may be for life. I know Jim is happy now and learning all that he can in the spirit world. I also feel in my heart that we have been together in past lives and will meet again in others. We are soul mates. Soul mates are not just for lovers anymore! Nope, your sister, your mother, your father—all could have been connected to you before. I think we know when we have that special connection with someone. It just feels bigger than this world. Jim comes to me in songs and through butterflies. Sometimes I will find his picture lying somewhere it wasn't before. I know he is with me, but man, I wish I could sit and chat with him again. We used to have the most amazing conversations. We would talk for hours about politics, philosophy, religion, spirituality, women, men, you name it we have probably discussed it. I know now that he is privy to so many more answers than I am and I wish with all my heart and soul I could spend an hour or two or a day with him again, face to face. My brother's passing taught me so much. It made me take a real look at my life. I am a caretaker. I like to help people if they need me. I love being a mother, a wife. I love working when my work and time and efforts help others to succeed with their passions. If I am not doing that kind of work I am not content.

Losing my brother taught me that I had put so much into his life, his care, his business that I lost track of me a bit. I am not complaining; I was there because he needed me. And in a sense I needed him to need me. After all, aren't we here to make a difference? I feel that true success is making a positive difference in someone's life. Nothing grandiose. Just reaching out to someone in need and helping. For no other reason than that they need help.

Think for a minute about how this world would be if everyone was living their passion, going through their days WANTING to make a positive difference in someone's life. Would we have war? Crime?

Divorce? Would we fight over who should be allowed to love whom and what church is the best? Would we spend our days angry at people that wronged us?

I don't think we would. I think this consciousness would instead breed universal peace and promote unity. Does this mean we would all think the same way? Geez . . . I hope not. My philosophy is that the reason we have so many choices and options in our world is that we NEED them. Why? Because we all need to believe in something. But we are not created to ALL believe in the same things. It just makes sense if you think about it. With all the different cultures, religions, political preferences, and mindsets in this world, how could we possibly think there is just ONE answer to any of these important questions? It's just a crazy concept to me.

A good friend emailed the other day and said that although she didn't share the same spiritual beliefs as me, she realized it was what gave me hope and helped me through. And she respected that. WOW! I wrote her back and said, "That is what true friendship is. Knowing you have differences and respecting that person anyway." Do we have to be right? Do we have to convert everyone to OUR way of thinking? No, man . . . what an exhausting job that would be. When we do, we come out sounding egotistical, pushy, judgmental, angry, and sometimes just mean.

I don't know about you, but that is not the way I want to make people feel. When religions start to judge and ostracize people, they create a division and guilt and upset. I can't believe the God that I know and love would want this. He doesn't want his love to be twisted until it fits the needs of others to use as a weapon to hurt people.

But those are just my beliefs. They may differ from yours and guess what? That is perfectly alright with me!

My Brother, the Thinker

July 2011. My brother Jim is 5 years older than me. I have always had a very special relationship with him. When we were young I was his shadow, following him around whenever he would let me. He helped with homework and talked with me when I had questions. I remember one day he even took me on a date with him and his girlfriend to the movies. I was like 8 and couldn't believe how cool he was. To this day I am not sure how his girlfriend felt about it though. When I was 10, Jim went away to Vermont Academy, a prep school in Vermont three long hours away. It was my first true heartbreak. I stayed in my room all weekend long, crying, feeling like my life was over. How could I go on without my big brother? Who would stick up for me when my other brothers picked on me? Who would help me with my homework? Who would answer my very important 10-year-old questions about life? I wrote him letters and sent him pictures but his short visits home just weren't the same. He had grown apart from me. I still looked up to him, still couldn't wait to be in his presence, but I felt the change. I felt it and it hurt.

From Vermont Academy, Jim went off to Yale University and then to New York City for a year before planning to start at the Yale School of Drama. I saw him less and less. One night as I was getting ready for bed the phone rang. Since it was nearing 10pm I knew it wasn't good news. Soon my stepdad, Ed, knocked on my bedroom door. He told me that Jim had been in a motorcycle accident and was hurt badly. He did not tell us that the hospital staff thought Jim would most likely be dead by the time we got there. We drove in the darkness from New

Jersey to Bellevue, the oldest hospital in the city. Being country people, Bellevue was a nightmare. (I guess even if you are not from the country Bellevue can be a nightmare.)

When we arrived at the ER, I looked around in utter amazement. There were prisoners strapped to chairs and bleeding from gunshot wounds, people moaning and crying and in shock. My mother was a mess and walked to the nurses' station to ask for my brother. The nurse was very harried and busy and not used to pleasantries. She told my mom that she didn't know where Jim was and she would just have to wait. I took one look at my mom's face and thought, *My little 5'6" petite-framed Italian Mother is going to take this huge city chick out!* I stepped in and said, with all of the confidence of a barely 16-year-old, "Please, we have come from New Jersey and we were told that my brother was hurt badly. My mother isn't trying to give you a hard time, we are just worried about my brother." She looked at me and then at my mom's angry face again and rechecked for Jim's name. She found it and directed us to the proper place. A lot of this night is shaky to me and I don't remember everything. I remember a doctor coming out to talk with my mom and her breaking down and crying when he told her that Jim had a multitude of injuries: broken front and back ribs, a punctured lung, a head injury with over one hundred stitches.

The deal breaker, though, was that his left leg had been run over by the city bus that hit him and the doctor wanted her permission to amputate the leg below the knee. Jim was an incredible athlete and while playing football for Yale was scouted by professional teams. He was young and had been an athlete almost all of his life. What would this mean to him? My mother had a horrible decision to make that night, one that my brother blamed her for, for most of the rest of his life. She asked the doctor what he would do if this was his child. He didn't hesitate to say that he'd amputate.

The bus had taken off most of Jim's lower left leg and half of his foot. They said that if they left the leg on Jim would never walk normal again and that he would be in constant pain. There was also the chance of infection and that the leg would have to be amputated anyway. He said if they did it now, they could amputate below the knee, which made having a prosthetic leg much easier. The doctor felt this would give Jim a chance at a real life where he could be physically productive again once he healed. My mom gave the go-ahead.

I was with Jim a week later when he came out of his coma. He looked at me and then down at where his leg should be and said only, "Jennie, go get Mom now." I was scared and hurting for him and I ran to get my mom. I don't remember the rest of that day, but I know it was a hard one for my Mom, and for my brother, to learn that life as he had known it was now changed forever. No more football. Would he be able to continue his stage acting? Would he finish school? So many questions, so many trials to come.

Fast forward several years later. I am back in New York City standing in a crowd of people watching runners go by in a marathon. I waited with my heart in my stomach to see Jim heading toward the finish line. It was his first big marathon ever. He had risen above his amputation and the attack the bus had done to his once healthy body and he was whole again, running with a prosthetic leg that still rubbed against his stump until it bled every time he ran. But he did it anyway, every day, training until he limped in pain. I heard my mom scream and looked up to see Jim coming in. He was running like a pro, smiling, and I started screaming his name. I screamed until my voice was hoarse and nearly gone. Tears streamed down my face as my best friend, my hero, crossed the finish line. We would find out later that Jim had not only defied death and a broken body to rise up and run a marathon, but he had broken a world record that day, putting many two-legged men to shame. I didn't care about that, even though Jim was elated. I only cared about the fact that my brother was alive and healthy and still in my life. I was always so very proud of him.

Jim went on to make a profession out of doing triathlons, getting sponsors like Bud Light and Silipos. He helped the Silipos Corporation design the gel inserts that amputees use to protect their stumps from the prosthetics. They went on to make so many useful items from the same material, such as bed pads to protect patients who are bedridden from sores. Jim also met Kirk Douglas when Kirk interviewed him for a book he was writing called *The Gift,* a novel about a bullfighter that lost his leg. Kirk wanted to get Jim's story and hear firsthand what it was like to be an amputee. Kirk soon was on a book tour and took Jim along. We went to see them both on *The Joan Rivers Show* in 1992. I met Kirk and he was a delight, but of course it was Jim I wanted to be with. I hadn't seen him for a while and I just wanted to be with him. We asked Jim to lunch after the show but he went off with Kirk instead. I was sad, but glad that I could see him for as long as I did.

Another Powerful Motivator Leaves the Earth

April 2012. Eighteen months after Jim's passing, our dear friend Sean O'Malley passed away. Just shy of his 41st birthday, he, like Jim, had spent most of his life inspiring others to live up to their potential. The creator of the Cardio Coach Guided Workout Series, he spent years perfecting ways to encourage people to get fit and live their passions. He was a good friend to Jim, and he looked up to him. But to me, Sean was a godsend—a support system and a lifeline. He helped me raise money for Jim's Choose Living Foundation and created Press Play Day, a global event held in January of 2008 to raise awareness and funds for Jim. On Press Play Day, thousands of people all over the world came together through their headphones to work out at the same time to an audio cardio challenge that Sean and Jim co-created. Even now, a dedicated group of over 150 fitness enthusiasts get together on the last Saturday of every month to exercise to the Press Play challenge or one of Sean's other CDs.

The Press Play workout features Sean's wonderful coaching voice and an intimate conversation with Jim. A renowned professional fitness trainer and spin instructor, Sean encouraged and promoted the ultimate performance from everyone he trained. The combination of these two great men was exceptional and powerful. It's not surprising that they were fast friends within minutes of meeting. In November of 2007, Sean and his business manager and friend, Karal, flew from Virginia Beach to San Diego to meet Jim, who happened to be in the hospital battling one of his bad UTI infections. They arrived late in the afternoon to find Jim lying in his bed, resting. The doctor in charge gave them 15 minutes to visit and scheduled a time to meet the next day for an interview.

Huddled in Jim's small room, they talked nonstop for the next two hours. It was as if they had known each other forever, and they became very close friends. When Jim passed, Sean cried with me. He flew to Pennsylvania and was there for me at Jim's Ceremony of Life. When he hugged me, I felt his strength and didn't want to let go. He was my protector after I had just lost the one real protector in my life. The real tragedy of Sean's passing is that he chose it. He battled depression for years, and although he was surrounded by so many that loved and supported and appreciated him, it wasn't enough. He took his own life to stop the pain his emotions invoked.

Sean, a man who touched so many and helped and inspired people all over the world, could not see his worth. That is the irony. A man whose life was a true success because he spent it touching others could not see his value to society, to me, to his family and friends.

I know that Jim met Sean on the other side and is helping him regroup. Sean will be okay because he is stronger than he ever knew. My heart breaks for his sister, my dear soul sister Colleen. She now has the battle and challenge of keeping his memory and earthly spirit alive. Like me, she doesn't want her loving, inspiring brother's light to leave this earth. Through her pain, it will survive and live on. Through her work, his death will never be in vain.

As I struggle to find the right words to share, I remember a time when I was down on myself, unsure if I had what it would take to do a job that had been put in my path. Jim sat with me and talked to me, encouraging me and strengthening me with his love. Assuring me and reminding me of all I had done for him in business and how I could accomplish even more if I put my mind to it. I think of that now. Doors have been closing in my life and I now await some new ones to open. The other day, I made the joke that if they didn't open soon I would start kicking them open . . . one by one!

I know Jim is waiting for me to do something here. I must do something to continue his message and his name. I have hidden behind my grief for far too long. I must for his sake, for my sake, break out of this box I am in and make things happen.

Touching Many Lives

May 2012. After Jim's passing, many of his friends came to me in person, by phone, and in emails to share how Jim had touched their lives. I was blown away by the stories. I was soon to find out that Jim was not just my protector, but throughout his life he was the protector of many.

One friend tells of meeting Jim on the lacrosse field after the other team had taken a disliking to him and decided to jump him during a play. He's pinned to the ground, but the next thing he knows, bodies are flying, and when he looks up, Jim's there yelling at the guys to "Get the hell off him!" Jim helped him up with a casual, "You OK, man?" This man never forgot what Jim had done for him, a younger teammate he really didn't even know. Jim had been the victim of bullies growing up and vowed never to let it happen to others. He kept that promise throughout his life.

The stories kept pouring in. How Jim had inspired them, helped them, protected them. One friend he had talked out of suicide. Think about that: Here is a man whose life is filled with trauma and tragedy and yet he continues to reach out and help others whenever he can. Was he perfect, this brother of mine? No. Not even close. But he lived a life full of love, and protection, and inspiration. That was worth so much to so many.

I have come to believe that Jim got up every day in order to live his passions. Without that ability, he probably wouldn't have ever gotten out of bed. His passions carried him through his life: First academics and sports, then acting, triathlons, and motivational speaking. Man, did he love to speak. To motivate. To make people laugh. I had the pleasure of traveling with Jim on several speaking jobs. I would help him get ready, do the sound checks, etc. As I sat in the audience watching rehearsal for the ESPYS, his intro video would make me cry every time—never failed. I'd be out there with everyone else in the audience crying, and even though I knew his story and watched his pain, that damn video got me every time. It broke my heart to see what he had gone through and was going through rehashed before everyone's eyes, but it was imperative for the audience to know his story. To know how he had come to be in this wheelchair in front of them. From here Jim felt he could move on to helping them know that they too could overcome anything life threw at them. They could reinvent themselves as he had and persevere. He loved to make them laugh with stories of how he had fallen out of his wheelchair and lain there until someone came for him.

I found these stories horrifying to hear, but Jim somehow made them funny and people could see past his disability to the man behind it. For aren't we all only human after all? Just people behind the costumes and the masks we wear? A few months, ago I was preparing a speech I was giving at a nearby college on Jim's life when it hit me. Why did Jim do what he did? How did Jim do what he did on a daily basis? How did he get past the pain, the upset, the anger? He did it by living his passions. So that became the tagline for my speech. I called it *Choose Living: The Jim MacLaren Story—Overcoming Adversity by Living Your Passions.* This really was Jim's message: That we all had it in us to overcome anything because we all had our passions inside to live. The trick is to know what makes you passionate. Do you know what your passions are? I have met people of all ages that have no clue. They forget what makes them excited, happy, and full of joy. They have succumbed to this life of hardship, work, stress, fear of not succeeding. Let's look at the word "successful." Can we really be successful if we are not living our passions? Are we being true to ourselves if we choose a life away from our passions? Are we even perhaps short-changing ourselves and those around us by not sharing the gifts that are our passions? Not tapping into what we are really destined to be doing? I believe we are—Yes! I think people that live their passions make more money, are more successful, and are happier and more fulfilled. Is it always easy to stay on this passion path? No, sometimes it is very hard. You hit walls. People who don't support you . . . they are there at every turn. They are the naysayers, the ones that are also not listening to their hearts and living their true self.

People that live their passions can sometimes frighten those that don't. Maybe it sets the bar a little higher for them and they are not interested in that. It makes them think about the years they have lost trying to figure out what makes them happy. I think the older we get the harder it is to remember our passions. That's why I feel it is essential for children to be taught to know and live their passions, whether the notions they have seem crazy to their parents or not. Help them embrace and learn and experience their passions as early as possible. It could be as easy as buying them a book on the subject, getting them singing or instrumental lessons, wherever their interests lie. Help them learn and experience them.

Even as adults we still have time. Until we leave this earth we have time to discover our passions. I have read that if you think back to what you liked to do, enjoy, dream about, when you were between the ages of 10 and 12, these thoughts can lead you to your passions. If you can't remember back that far, perhaps ask your family members or longtime friends what they recall. If that's not an option, you might have to start the search on your own. Start by thinking about your interests. If you had all the money and time in the world, what would you do? Where would you go? If you could work any job possible what would it be? Where would you live if you could choose any place in the world? Start journaling your answers. As you write, your soul will start to remember what brings it joy. Take some short classes, make a trip to the library and take out some books of interest. Learn a new language. Whatever it takes to break your mind out of the box it's been in. Allow it to reinvent itself into the thinking powerhouse you need it to be. The thing to remember is that it is never too late to be happy, to live your passions, to become the person you were destined to be.

If it takes you months or years to figure out what your passions are, don't fear. You will remember. It will be in that paragraph you read, that news report on TV, that picture you see. Remain open and the answers will come. You may find you are already dabbling in a passion but perhaps not living up to it the way you desire. Either way, the time has come. Anyone reading this can find happiness, joy, and peace within themselves by discovering and acknowledging all that you have within you—and all of us have passions within us. Don't start thinking that you were just busy on Passion Handout Day, that you missed it.

Nope! That's never the case. We all have gifts. We have simply allowed life to push them down and make them unimportant or hard to remember. But they are there. Of this I am certain.

Let me give you an example. I have been writing since I was a child. First poems, then stories. I have cupboards full of completed notebooks. Lots of romantic relationship stories that I wrote strictly for myself because I liked to write and read them. I always figured no one else would have an interest in them, and that didn't matter to me. Why? Because it was a passion. I write because I enjoy writing. Not so others can read it but because I enjoy doing it. Through the years I have come to wonder if perhaps I am supposed to be using that passion to do more than store notebooks in my cupboard. My children have said to me over the years, as they watched me get lost in my writing, "Mom, why don't you sell your books?" My answer was always, "Who would want to read these?" But then I started to think. Maybe someone might want to read them. Perhaps that is why I have been writing for so many years, to share with others and not just myself. Our passions are not meant for us to keep hidden. We do a disservice to ourselves and others that way.

Our passions are meant to be explored and shared, because passions are for the good of all that experience them. We feel this when we are touched by music or art or enjoy an incredible meal prepared by someone who loves to cook and is great at it. Or we read a book that we can't seem to get off our minds. Do you see how passions continue to give? When Jim gave his talks he touched so many. Sometimes he would touch someone countries away by giving an interview on TV. In the case of Emmanuel, Jim reached all the way to Ghana with his message and inspired Emmanuel to live his passions and bring awareness to the special gifts disabled people bring to this world, to show his country that disabled people were just as important as any other person and that they deserved the same rights and respect. If Jim had not reached out and let his voice be heard, a country oceans away would not have changed their laws and rights for their disabled people. People who had crawled and begged their whole life for food would not have felt that glorious moment when they crawled up into their new wheelchair. *All because someone here in the states cared enough to share it with them.*

Passions—it's what made Jim get out of bed every morning, and that was not an easy feat. It would take Jim close to three hours to get ready each day. He had a special bowel program that had to be done. He had to get his body through the pain that engulfed him daily. Just brushing his teeth took 15 minutes because his hands had developed contracture deformities and could not move like yours and mine. Jim had just enough feeling in his paralyzed body to feel pain constantly. It was a curse and a blessing. That he could feel at all was the blessing after being told he would never feel or move from the neck down again. But the pain would at times threaten to destroy him. It knocked him down, caused him to be addicted to painkillers, tried to steal his mind and at time his hope. But Jim continued to persevere. He would have his down days, cloistered in his darkened apartment with the quilt pulled up over his head. At those times, he wouldn't talk or interact . . . he was lost in his head. I think he was regrouping, gaining much-needed strength so he could come back stronger and teach some more. Share some more. Don't we all need that, that downtime? That time to just be in our own heads and close out the noise of others? The problem is, most of us don't take that time, and it becomes very apparent when life starts to overwhelm us. We don't sleep, eat, or function properly. So perhaps Jim had the right idea all along. Perhaps we all need those days when we stay in the dark and pull the quilt over our heads. Just another lesson Jim's challenges have taught us.

Grief

July 2012. It wasn't until recently that it came to my attention that I had not grieved for my brother. Don't get me wrong—I've had my moments of complete meltdown. But I haven't really allowed myself to go through the whole process. The guilt was there: Was I there for him enough? Why did I text him the night he died instead of going by or calling him? Why didn't I take more time to just sit with him instead of always rushing around trying to get everything done? I suddenly realized that every time my body tried to grieve, I would push it back. Distract myself with work, family, whatever. It is now coming to a head because you can't suppress grief forever. Especially something this great. This BIG.

I decided I needed help so I started seeing a counselor, a woman named Cindy who really got me. If I wasn't seeing her professionally, I would totally hang and have wine with her. Just a cool individual. She started to help me see the errors of my grieving ways. I just wasn't doing it. Every now and then after drinking or seeing a movie or hearing a song, I would lose it, but then those around me couldn't deal with it. So I would go and hide. Drive for hours crying. Go to the local park, sit, and cry. Then I would come back home and pretend nothing was wrong, take care of business, when all I wanted to do was get in my car and go away. Or I would never get out of bed in the first place. Sometimes late at night I would sit on the bathroom floor and cry and just remind myself how to breathe. I would be crying so hard that I could not catch my breath.

But there were people to care for and money to make. I had no choice but to perform because it is in my makeup to do so. It was a few months later that Cindy said to me, "You sound very angry at yourself." I turned to her and my eyes filled. She was so right. I was beyond angry. I was not a person who wallowed. I was strong. I took care of me and others and made things happen. But I knew I was falling short lately. Just the night before I had been driving in my car and I found myself screaming "FUCK YOU!" as loud as I could over and over, hitting the steering wheel until my wrists were bruised. I would find myself hitting walls as hard as I could just to feel any pain beyond what I was experiencing over losing Jim.

I finally had my daughter Sage design a tattoo for me. I had tossed around getting one since I turned 40 but kept chickening out. I couldn't come up with the symbol I wanted on my body for the rest of my life, but after Jim died, after the pain started to refuse to be ignored, I knew I would get a tattoo and it would be for Jim. It would be part of his legacy. I decided I wanted a butterfly to symbolize the awakening of the psyche, as we are both so into philosophy. I wanted to use the teal blue color of the Choose Living Foundation logo, and I wanted it to say "bro." That was what he always called himself to me. "Hey sis, it's your bro!" So Sage came up with the design, and on a day that I felt heavy with grief I went and had the tattoo done. It was the strangest thing—it hurt but I relished the physical pain. It fought the emotional pain that threatened to engulf me daily. It was also empowering because I got it despite knowing that many of my friends and family weren't behind it. It was something I did just for me and no one else. And it felt wonderful!

Another Loss for August

August 2013. Our Dad passed away on Saturday, August 3. Ironically enough, he left us the same month you did, Jim. I guess if you're to have a sad month, you might as well get all the sad stuff out of the way all at once instead of dragging it out through the year. I know that Dad started to have issues after your death. He felt so much guilt over you. He loved you so much but was so upset that he missed so much of your life due to the divorce and us being adopted by our stepdad. I often told him that the guilt was not necessary, that we had a good life with Robert and we now could be connected to him, as well. Things happen in our lives as they should. Sometimes they don't make any sense, but they are as they should be. Driving home the Thursday before Dad died, I got this overwhelming surge of emotions. It came out of nowhere and hit hard. I just started crying without control. I almost pulled over, thinking, "What the hell is going on?"

After it passed I knew that Dad had turned a corner and was letting go. He was letting me know. Or maybe it was you letting me know. It doesn't matter. The connection was made and life as I know it was about to change. So many changes this year. My marriage, my kids, Dad's death, new jobs, new passions in my life. The list of changes goes on and on. It brings with it many things. Chaos is one. Everywhere you turn it presents itself. Excitement is another. Change can be very exciting and scary all at once. I try not to let fears stop me from doing anything. I learned that from you bro. I have fears . . . oh boy, do I have them! But I make myself push past them. It is the only way for growth to take place. And I so want to grow. I want to be the very best I can be. I want to help others and really make a difference in this world. As I watch people I love pass over, you and Sean and now Dad, I see that what really truly is left behind is the love we gave to others. It's what is remembered and embraced. I want to leave a lot of love behind. I want to do your legacies proud.

August 30th, 2013. The anniversary of your death. Three long years without your smile, your intelligence, your light in my daily life. I recently moved into my own apartment, my first time ever being alone. The place is full of your stuff and mine. I hung your picture in the living room and I talk to you daily. On move-in day I told you, "It's our place Bro!" I realized today as I touched your picture when I left the house that I can look at your photos now.

The Connecting of Spirits

October 2013. Through the last year and a half, my life has seen many changes: A separation from my husband of 22 years, a loss of family time, and the loss of my dad, James Edward Snow. New relationships, new places to live. So much in such a short time.

About a year ago I reunited with a strong spirit, a man I knew long ago. He reminded me of Jim in many ways. He too was full of passion and light and anger. My brother Jim carried so much anger. Not too hard to understand given the challenges in his life. But this anger often got in the way of the light waiting to shine on Jim. With my friend I felt the same intuitive thoughts, he was dealing with the same anger. I wanted to help him see the light. I wanted to care for him and show him the world had much love to offer and he was deserving of it. I struggled with the whole thing, but the fact that he reminded me of Jim kept me going back time after time. Every time he closed a door I banged on it until he opened it again. I continued loving, trying. I know this sounds strange, and I can't explain it any more than I have. The connection I felt with this man overwhelmed me, taking over my rational thoughts and distracting me beyond distraction. I finally learned that his anger, turned abusive with me, was a demon I could not fix. He had his own work to do and he was not filled with the love my brother had, and no amount of love from me would be able to heal him. And beyond that, when our goal to help someone becomes detrimental to us it is time to move on.

The reason for this connection, this relationship, this lesson, has yet to show itself. Sometimes I feel it never will. But he remains what he always will be: a connection to Jim, a deep, deep connection to me. When I love I take it seriously. Even when hurt by others, if I loved you at any time it stays. With some I love deeper than others. That is often a cause of distress. For some being loved so deeply can be too much to take. But it is something inside of me. It's part of my spirit. Something I think I have carried with me through lifetime after lifetime. I think my challenge is to be able to balance the love so that it doesn't come to my own demise. I am still working on that one. It is why the loss of Jim has consumed my world. The love I have goes on and on and makes living my life like before his death impossible. Again the battle continues on to find the balance. To love and let go so that life, and the things determined to go on in my life, continue without restraint. This I feel will be my most difficult journey, but one I must complete.

So many people have come into my life via Jim. Connections through his speaking, his schools, and friends he has had for years and years. They have embraced me, supported me, loved me. I have friends on Facebook I only know through Jim. I haven't even met most of them but there were nights I was up alone, very late grieving, missing Jim, and they were there for me. With written support, quotes, love. Jim continues to lend me support even from beyond. He knows me. More than anyone else ever has. I believe he keeps sending people to support me and will until I no longer need the support. I am so very grateful for the support system in my life. I know I have been blessed with so many good people. It still amazes me how knowing this I can still have moments of intense loneliness. But then there are those that can still feel lonely in a sea of people. Because the parts that are lonely are the parts we hide from others. Overcoming this feeling is just part of the journey.

The Final Chapter

August 2014. For many moons now I have been functioning in a world within the world. It has been a strange, wild trip. Trying hard to be someone I can be proud of. Trying hard to help and serve others. Trying so hard to be a good mom and make up for the separation I have put them through. I gave my love to another man after I separated from my husband; gave him a little piece of my soul, but he didn't want it and threw it back. But it doesn't work that way. You can't give something like that back. It just leaves a break, a fracture in the soul. I don't understand why I gifted it in the first place. Why I allowed myself to love when my love was not wanted.

Perhaps because the soul knows more than the heart or the brain. I still love. Deep. It doesn't go away for me. If it comes back I am full of joy. If it doesn't, I remain in love with the soul connection.

Jim, I remain lost without you. You and I, we just understood each other. You would know by a sound in my voice or a look on my face that I was hurting. I knew the same with you. This connection we have makes you leaving the earth so much more hurtful. I know you get it now, you have remembered it all, your path, your goals, your mission that extends way beyond what we acknowledge here on earth. But even though I know there is so much more than this, I hurt, needing our connection in real time. I am moving forward, trying to build a life within all the changes. I will be all that I can be, because otherwise I am wasting my time here on earth. I know you understand that. Sometimes the loneliness threatens to consume me—being in a sea of people and feeling nothing but empty and sad. The feeling doesn't last forever and I force myself to do something positive and proactive. I am not a good sad person. I love life, people, I love loving. It fills me with joy to have love for others. I love to do nice things for people. To see others happy. I love to be with my children and listen to them as they express their passions and thoughts on things that are important to them. I know you love them so much, too. My kids were so important to you. You were so good to them. I also know that you are around them still today, watching out for them when I can't. Honestly, what a blessing that is. I know in my heart that your spirit is alive and well.

I know I have no reason to be sad. But I am. You and I discussed everything and anything. I loved your mind. So full of EVERYTHING. Sometimes I think you had so much in there that you didn't know what to think about or share first. You had so many passions.

You were so full of life even when your physical body let you down. You could be so stubborn and angry sometimes but then you could just push it all aside and do something fabulous and generous for someone. Sometimes a total stranger. I have that in me, too. I just love making someone feel loved and happy. I love to see the light that comes from someone who has been lifted up. It is such a beautiful thing. You loved that too. I think enjoying the happiness of others is a blessing. Sometimes you were this incredibly spiritual man. Your heart was so big it threatened to expand outside of your chest. Other times you closed yourself up—stopping relationships that were filling you with love. You hid from the commitment that a loving relationship can bring, so spiritual and so very human all at the same time. I feel the same sometimes. Sometimes I feel I can't function here because my passions sometimes scare people away. I am intense. I am sincere and willing to give almost all of me to the right person. It is my greatest strength and also my greatest weakness. You can never give all of yourself to anyone. You can't give away all of your energy, all of yourself. Because then what are you left with? I have been known to do that. One day you wake up and realize there's nothing left of you. It's no one's fault; most people will take what is offered to them, never thinking it is hurting the other person. It is our job to monitor ourselves. To create and keep the balance so that our strengths, which I believe we are meant to share with each other, do not become our own demise. Every choice I made was mine. I blame no one for anything negative that happened in my life. The people that hurt me, I allowed them in, I made the choice to have them be present in my life. It was up to me to change things so that only positive remained.

You taught me so much, but one of the biggest things was that no matter how down and out things are, no matter how hopeless things seem to be, there is an answer. There is a way to prevail and go on to be bigger and better than before. So in my darkest moments I know I won't wallow long. The learning is in the process. The growth is in the recovery.

Your greatest gift to me was all that I have mentioned. Love freely, give often, use your challenges to excel and help others. Take what this life dishes out and make it something great! Something worthwhile. The greatest fears I have are these: That your memories will fade for this world. That your spirit, your passions, will be forgotten as people engulf themselves in this world of fear, lost love, challenges. That your lifetime here will be for naught. My goal is to make sure that doesn't happen, to create this written tribute to the man who protected me in this lifetime, the man I protected with all of my inner strength and wisdom. The man I have known before in lifetimes of known and unknown stories. The man I will see again and thrive with and learn from. The other thing I fear is that I will not live up to all I know I must. That I might ignore the plan I chose for myself before taking on this human form. To not help all that I can while I am able. But fears as you know are of the human race. Our souls know no boundaries, no limits. Our souls know our paths. In this lifetime and beyond, to ignore our souls is the greatest tragedy. You have taught me so much my brother, my soulmate, in your human ways and the ways of your soul. Together we continue to walk the path. Sometimes our paths will cross and at other times we will walk alone. All is well. All is well. My heart remains in awe of you. My love continues to grow each day for you. My soul reaches out to you daily. Awaiting the time when we meet again.

There is so much happening and so many challenges presenting themselves, there isn't a day that goes by when I don't physically and emotionally miss you. Your picture hangs on my wall and you look so very much alive. It hurts me to see it, and it helps me to see it every day. You are such a part of me that existing without you at full capacity has proven very difficult. My brain knows I must but my soul fights it with all its might. It's like two parts of a whole and one part is just not there. It makes no sense so I have trouble grasping it. Things have to make sense to me or I fight it. I am fundraising to self-publish this book. It is slow but I will make it happen somehow. What is my choice? I must! It is written in the stars; it was written before this lifetime occurred. I need to get it into print. Connections like ours transcend lifetimes. So hard for some to understand, it just takes on a life of its own. I want your memory, your message, to go on and on. Every time someone sees one of your videos they are floored. You have touched people over and over. I can't tell you how blessed I am that you were in my life, and I know you were before. Some people understand that and some don't. But what is, is. I don't mess with the details, I just know it's real. Yesterday I was rereading a message from our dear friend Sean. He was another great loss to this world. He never realized his great worth, his value. So strange when so many others saw his strength and drew from it daily. It breaks my heart that he left the earth never understanding his impact on others. After you passed, Sean was my rock. He knew you and me so deeply. He reached out to me and supported me and then, like you, he left. He left behind so many who relied on him, needed him still. Yet Sean always felt so very alone. Isn't that the ultimate depression? You feel like there is no hope, no point to stay here any longer. You are so self-absorbed that all others around you just disappear. If I had been on his call list the night Sean took his life I would have tried to renew his strength, but I know others that loved him dearly had tried over and over. And if this was his path then he would have just chosen another time to leave. Our path is our path. I wonder, did he cut his short or did he complete it for this lifetime? A question I would love to ask him sometime, just one of life's many questions.

I know you are beyond here now. You are working your magic bringing people into my life that help and support. They keep lifting me up, back to performance level. Some days that is such a great challenge to me. I thank you for helping me, Bro. You now realize that all this doesn't matter, but you know it still does to me. It consumes me and lies so heavy on my shoulders that sometimes I feel I might crumble, just disengage until there is nothing left of me. I have always been engulfed in others, trying to lift and support them, and then suddenly you were gone. The kids are growing older and more self-sufficient. Of course, this is what I have always wanted for them. But it is a change. I seemed to wake one day a fractured soul, disjointed by loss and change. It reminds me of the fall, when things die off and winter sets in making room for spring and rebirth. This is my soul, empty in parts, waiting for the spaces to be filled. I find myself consumed by emotions that threaten to stop my breath, yet knowing deep inside that the mysteries are fighting to be discovered. They patiently wait as I fumble through life's ecstasies, embracing distractions at every turn. Your passing created space for my soul to grow, expand, and take others in. Tragic, terrifying, exciting, powerful but so very real. So very unwilling to be denied. The questions float around me, engulfing me in indecision and complacency. I know complacency is not an option for me, only acceptance is.

Acceptance is such a positive word, so often fought and ignored. Like the movies I watch, I need a happy ending, the satisfaction of loving and being loved. It is not a fantasy: it's my deepest, seeded need. Needs—not wants—must be fulfilled. I believe you deny your very essence if you don't, and that is the greatest sin. We cannot be totally happy if we deny ourselves our path, our essence. You taught me that, Bro. A good friend of yours wrote me after you came to her during a meditation in her Zen garden. She said that you said to tell me that you now know that LOVE is everything. To love and be loved is the answer to all of life's questions. Then you went on to tell her that you wished you had done more loving while here on earth. I will share your message with all who will listen. This book is for you, it is part of your memoirs, part of both of our paths. I hope I have done you justice. I love you.

6 POEMS FOR MY BROTHER, FROM MY HEART
by Jennifer Hippensteel

#1

I woke up today, deep in the pain, wondering all the while.

What did we learn, what did we seek, when will we meet again?

What is your path, will it connect with mine sometime soon?

What are my goals now that you're gone, will it all come out all right?

Where is the person I used to be, the one whose life was filled with you?

The empty hole you left for me continues to grow each day.

Such a weird thing when I am so blessed with so much, to contemplate the emptiness.

I know that though our paths crossed your path is your own. It's selfish of me to want that to change.

Perhaps you can take just a few minutes and visit me again.

Remind me of what the hell the new plan is.

I watch for your signs, they come now and then and the tears start to fall.

Please don't take that to mean I don't want you here, I live for them all.

I feel in my heart we will meet again, please make sure I am aware.

The only thing that is clear in my present life is how very much I care.

#2

The heart . . . all knowing . . . all feeling . . . engaged.

It reacts at will . . . randomly . . . with forethought or with spontaneity.

It feels immense joy . . . incredible pain. . . . Without a need for justification it cries out for acceptance.

It needs its love returned. Or it weeps with hurt . . . threatens to break apart.

The heart . . . it knows no boundaries . . . it refuses to die.

The heart . . . beats for many . . . or for just one . . . but when it refuses to beat for love

The heart . . . will beat no more.

#3

I am lost, swimming in a pool of information without clarity.

I am found with passions that rock my existence.

I am lost with feelings that shouldn't be.

I am found with new connections that set me free.

I am lost with grief that continues to rock my daily life.

I am found with the knowledge that soul mates always meet again.

I am lost with the thoughts that flood my mind late at night.

I am found with the realization that morning sometimes brings light.

I am lost with the desires that feed off of my loneliness.

I am found with the fantasies my mind seems to find.

I am . . . lost and yet . . . found enough to make some sort of sick, crazy sense . . . of this life I live.

For that I am thankful.

#4

So many thoughts

So much emotion

Too many regrets

My mind's in constant motion

Love, lust, desire, satisfaction

I wait anticipating your reaction

Watching the clouds cover the sun

Rain pouring down, sadness has won

Tears on my pillow, barely awake

Desperately trying for everyone's sake

Finding the silence, it lies deep inside

After all this time there's no place to hide

Walking, working ignoring the pain

I fight each day to remain ever sane

The purpose I know lies in your success

I try every day not to digress

Peace, a feeling I try so hard to obtain

Suffering in silence, as my half empty heart remains

#5

Today is your birthday

My mind is full of memories of you

Laughing, joking, singing to me

Your smile would light up the room

You could always make me laugh with your impressions

You'd make me angry with your stubbornness, but then I have that too

You would try to lift me up when I was down

We could talk about anything and we did

My focus is off, my mind so full, my heart so sad

Come close, come quick, don't let me be

#6

Often, lost in this dark abyss

Struggling to keep my head above the warm, flowing waters, feeling at risk

Demanding, juggling, struggling, just trying to maintain

This story we live from day to day

Seeing light in places where none should be

Wondering what exactly that means for me

Desires invade my waking hours and tempt me as I sleep

Loneliness can come to call at any time, leaving me to weep

Blessings come and then they go

What do they mean? I need to know

The resentments I once carried are dissolving day by day

I only want the light to come and stay

There seems to be enough energy for only the light

I can't explain it . . . it just feels right.

#7

I am completely freaking out . . .

I am having trouble catching my breath.

I think I have come to the end of the line.

I called a counselor this morning, I hope it helps.

I must get through this. I must figure out my life.

What I need, want, desire.

What's right for me, wrong for me.

How to make changes without hurting others.

If a person can be broken, I am.

How to fix me? How? How? How?

I just want to run and run and run until I hit the wall.

Trying to focus while I catch my breath.

It's so damn hard to catch my breath.

#8

Climbing, climbing trying to escape the abyss

And its incredible pull

Searching, longing for that something just beyond my reach

I reach out and find it's only air I grasp

This world we live in . . . Full of chaos and thrills

Take me back to a day when it all made sense

When I lived my will

Breathing in satisfaction and balance

Filling my days with the paths of those that I held close

Paths that led to something I could understand

Something that made sense to my spirit and mind

But now the path is unclear

Where does it lead?

Which is my path?

Where will it lead?

Who will get left behind?

I pray it isn't me

7 IN HIS OWN WORDS
From Jim's unpublished manuscript
The Power of Being Alive: The Eternal Wellspring of the Spirit

I always like to show a video clip of my story before I go on stage to speak to an audience. It gets my story out of the way right away and then I can spend more time talking about what we have in common when I'm in front of the audience.

Although I have to admit I have always shown the best news piece at the time and my favorite is my acceptance speech from the ESPY awards. Even though I've seen it 100 times I always watch it like it's the first time and sometimes I think, *wow, that's a pretty cool guy*. And then I remember that it's about me and I remind myself of what an idiot I could be sometimes. But does it seem like that? The times when we must feel like rock stars life somehow slaps us in the head and reminds us that we're just human beings. I get sick a lot with bladder infections and there are very few nights when I feel like I have enough energy to go out on a date. On one occasion I was living in La Jolla, California and for those of you who don't know it's a pretty wealthy area in Southern California. So I'm decked out in my black shirt and slacks and hanging out at a restaurant with my date and I'm feeling pretty cool, having sushi at the bar and hanging out with the beautiful people. However, when I'm wheeling back to valet parking I hand the attendant my ticket stub and as I look down at my legs I realize that I have both white dinner napkins strewn across my lap: not so cool.

I also remember a beautiful sunny day in Pasadena, California where I was living for a time while getting my master's degree and Ph.D. at Pacifica Graduate Institute. I had an appointment earlier in the day so I was dressed up in my elegant Italian slacks and shirt. I had just had a long conversation with a writer at GQ magazine and she told me that she was going to fly out for five days and spend time writing a major article on me. So I'm wheeling down the street. It's about lunchtime so all the corporate types are sitting at the outside café enjoy their lunches and there is a lot of foot traffic. As I approach this alleyway, which I frequently used to cut through when there was a large amount of people walking on the Main Street, I notice that the chain is down so I start to wheel over the chain. But I've forgotten that I was in a different wheelchair than usual. This wheelchair had a center wheel drive cell so it got caught on the chain and here goes MacLaren flying through the air about 20 feet. My catheter bag comes undone, my artificial leg falls off right in front of the entire crowd sitting at the outside café. Well, I don't know if you've ever been in an accident or fallen, but you get an adrenaline rush for about five minutes. So for five minutes I'm the funniest guy alive when I fall from my chair. I looked like an insect on its back, thinking while I can't get up, "where's my clapper? "About four or five large-size men got up from the tables at the café and lifted me up to put me back in my wheelchair. One of them grabbed my artificial leg and wasn't quite sure what to do with it, my catheter bag was collected from over there and handed to me. I thank them all profusely and still had that adrenaline rush so I was cracking jokes etc. but when I wheeled over into a quiet corner in the alley the adrenaline had worn off and I realized that I hurt. I don't have the muscular physique that I had as a triathlete and so when I fall, I hurt. Beyond that, it's also a great time for reflection, reminding myself that I'm human.

Doesn't it seem like this happens to all of us? We feel superhuman and then life throws something at us. In my case with two near-fatal accidents I guess it took two bricks being thrown at me to get it.

It took me quite a long time looking for the answer within myself, as to whether you had to do it with big bricks like losing a leg and then breaking a neck to understand that we are just human. But I've come to the conclusion through my own experiences it doesn't take something that tragic to get it. Socrates said, "an unexamined life is a life not worth living." It's my experience that we all live in a wheelchair in one way or another. Our "stuff" is our "stuff" and although your stuff may seem pale in comparison to what happened to me, it's still your stuff to deal with. I'm often asked why I had two accidents and I reply, "maybe I just needed to sit down." Although I'm being slightly humorous I kind of mean it. I have time to do something that in this fast-paced world many of us don't: take the time to reflect. And also it can be a scary process. Living an examined life means nothing if we can't look at those parts of ourselves that we might feel unashamed of or vulnerable about. I don't think of myself as a teacher. All that I can do is share my own experiences. That's all I really know, my own experiences. But I'll tell you that by looking at all aspects of ourselves, not just cocktail party chatting about what we do etc. but really looking at what we feel are weaknesses, in doing this we actually become better human beings. I don't mean better as in better than someone else. I can guarantee you that you will be more fulfilled and quite frankly, happier.

Truly, how can we live our lives without knowing who we really are, the good and the bad. Without knowing ourselves we are like a pinball machine where each day a handle with a spring is pulled back launching us into our day. Then we are the pinball bouncing off each bumper. For me, the bumpers represent people and the experiences we have with them throughout our day—if we don't know who we are and we just react to people from our emotions and not from our center. For me the game, or the day if you will, takes place underneath the board in that huge black space. Living in that space lets me invent my entire day. I mean, think about it. If you do a project at work or at school and 20 people are waiting in line to comment on your project, 19 of them will walk up to you and say "Wow, it was amazing. And it's the most incredible thing I've ever seen you do." Then the 20th person comes up and says "That that was the worst work I have ever seen you do." I wonder how many of us will let that 20th person ruin the rest of our day? Let's backtrack. What really happened? Nineteen people liked what you did and one person didn't like it. Okay, that's what happened—so let's just move on. But why do we do this? Why do we let one person ruin the rest of our day? Who knows, they've probably just had a bad breakfast.

Emotions are wonderful things. We love to feel good, psyched, love. But without knowing who we are we let our emotions run us and usually we tend to let the negative emotions make the strongest impression on us. Why do we do this? We self-destruct ourselves and yet we are the strongest advocates for ourselves.

Think about how most of us wake up each morning. We hit the snooze alarm button and immediately our brains starts racing: "Oh my God the money for my kids at school." Or we have problems with our spouses or significant others, or we lift up the sheet and say "Oh my god I'm fat!" and then we know we don't want to but we have to look in the mirror as we go by and then it's, "Oh my god I'm *really* fat!" We've already started to self-destruct ourselves and we haven't even begun the difficult part of our day.

In my experience there is a better way. Do you know that time when you first wake in the morning, right in the moment where you're not quite awake but not quite asleep either? It's a kind of ethereal feeling where we're not quite worried about anything, we're not fat yet, or not in a wheelchair yet. I try and take just five minutes during this time to think about something that makes me feel good about myself. And I don't care if it's the $50,000 Ferrari that you want. Just think about something that makes you feel happy. Then what we've done is given ourselves a tool to use for the rest of our day. And you don't have to act like a Buddha or go off in a corner and close your eyes to meditate.

You can be in the middle of a board meeting or in class and all you need to do is reflect upon that five-minute period of earlier in the day. So no matter where you are sitting even with your eyes open you have reconnected yourself with yourself. And suddenly you're centered again and able to handle whatever is being thrown at you. This is a tool that I often use several times a day. And the best part is: it works!

Fall in love with being *alive*. We are the artists; change the color, change the painting, change your mind and change your Life.

There is a line in the movie *The Thin Red Line* that is spoken to a group of new army recruits as the veterans coming back from battle walk by: "You don't start with courage, first you do the thing that you're afraid of and then you get the courage."

In my experience there is nothing more true than this one simple line. We are not born courageous; it's not a gift that is given. We do have to face what we're afraid of and then the courage comes after. There are often things in life that are just indescribable until you go through them. Breaking my neck was not only a tragedy with the gifts to come afterwards but it was a learning experience as well as multiple opportunities to do what I was afraid of and then at some point the courage would eventually come.

I spent nearly 6 months at the Craig Hospital for Rehabilitation. Not only is it one of the finest facilities in the world, their human beings who work with you, the nurses all the way down to the caregivers, were just incredible. Monday through Friday I got to spend my time with the same staff and became very accustomed to working with them. The weekends were a mixed bag because I would get a different caregiver and a different nurse so that the Monday to Friday shift could get some time off. Truthfully one of the scariest things I had to deal with on Saturday every week was this one male caregiver who would shave my face, as I was unable at that time to move any part of my body. It was a single-edged razor and I'm telling you it was one of the scariest parts of the entire event.

But let me tell you there were times when I was really afraid. When I woke up from the first of many surgeries that week, I had a metal screw in the back of my head attached to a line that held a weight down to the floor. This was done so that I was unable to move my neck before they put a medieval device that they call a halo on my head and chest.

A halo is nothing like it sounds. It's a metal contraption attached to a huge plastic chest plate. The doctor screws four long bolts into your skull that are attached to four vertical metal shafts that are attached to the plastic plate that rests upon your chest. In this way you are completely unable to move your neck. At this point after the accident I was unable to move anything anyway. And one other thing, they don't use anesthetic when they put on the halo and so it's pretty painful. At some point during my month-long stay in the ICU doctors discovered a clot in my neck. So they had to take the halo off and perform a 13-hour surgery to remove the clot, put a metal plate on the back of my vertebrae, and fuse part of my hip bone to the front of my neck. I was on my stomach for 13 hours with my jaw jutting out. The TMJ that resulted was so severe that I had to drink pureed food from a straw for the next three months. A day or so after the surgeries—at this point I was sleeping only one hour per night so things were pretty timeless—but I think it was a day or two after the surgery, the doctor had to put another halo on my head.

When I was in the ambulance on the way to the hospital after the collision with the van, I actually wasn't afraid. I knew that my legs didn't move but I was still in that adrenaline triathlon mind and body state so I thought to myself, *oh maybe I'm only a paraplegic so I'll be able to wheelchair race in the marathons and beat those guys.* Then once I arrived at the hospital, as I was lying on a stretcher outside of the operating area, a very kind soft-faced doctor was holding my hand. I couldn't really feel him holding onto my hand; the kindness in his eyes and just his energy made me feel safe. I felt like I would be okay if he never let my hand go. He had already told me I was a quadriplegic and would never move from the neck down for the rest of my life but it didn't seem real while he was holding my hand. Of course then the nurses came to wheel me into my first surgery and he had to let go of my hand, because now I was being wheeled into an entirely new life.

Perspective

I get sick a lot: this morning I awoke with a toxic feeling in my stomach, a headache, and just a general feeling of malaise. Often these sicknesses are related to my bladder and an infection. I've had so many IV needles stuck in my arm for antibiotics that I am immune to all oral antibiotics. It's days like today when I wake up in all of the pain that I usually have. These are really the days where perspective is truly needed. Even on a normal day when I wake with such incredible pain that I don't even have a word for it I often need to remind myself that the way I feel at that moment does not mean that the rest of my day will be the same. If I thought that way I would never get out of bed. But then I get days like today when there is an added layer of sickness. But again, to put it in perspective I still remind myself that the rest of the day is not necessarily going to feel like I am right now.

I guess I really haven't mentioned the pain I wake up with every morning. I love words. But due to recent surgeries and procedures I don't really have a word for how much pain I wake up with now. For the first 13 years after becoming a quadriplegic, when I awoke my body felt like wet cement plugged into a wall. Over the past two years I've had to get a skin graft on my right thigh after a restaurant served me such hot coffee that the top blew off just as I was sipping it. It caused third-degree burns on my hip and also a third-degree pressure wound. Pressure wounds are fairly common in those who are paralyzed. For those who are considered a complete injury, doing weights shifts in a wheelchair and being turned every few hours in bed while sleeping is also necessary to prevent them from occurring. A "complete" injury simply means that you will get no sensory or motor skills below the level of your injury.

Originally I was diagnosed a complete quadriplegic at the C-5, C-6 cervical levels. I was told I would be able to shrug my shoulders and bend my biceps. At some point during the first few months of my rehabilitation, I had a sensation in an area on the left side of my belly. Simply put, that little bit of sensation rendered me with a new identification: I was then considered an "INCOMPLETE" quadriplegic. I have to say I find it pretty humorous that I was now considered incomplete. The facts of paralysis are not related to the ways in which we usually think of retaining our strengths or "getting better." Nerves don't react to the kind of goal setting that we practice in our daily lives. If you're doing a project for class or training for a marathon, you start at X with the goal being Z. So we simply map out our course or the letter Y. Nerves don't act this way. My "incompleteness" could have stopped with the sensation in my lower belly. However, I reveled in this new sensation. Each morning the nurse came in to give me my blood thinning shots so that I would not get any clots in my body. She would ask me if I wanted the shot in my leg where I could not feel anything or if I wanted it in my belly. It was an easy answer; I wanted to feel so I always asked her to give me the shot in my lower belly. The simple fact was that the small amount of sensation might be the end of it. There are some reactions to the XYZ training program, but if a nerve does not enervate to an area of the body, then that muscle movement and/or sensation will not occur.

The Gift of Being Alive

It's morning on a Wednesday. Actually it's a morning like any other day; waking up in much pain, thoughts beginning to acknowledge the pain that my body is in. I start drinking water to try and keep my catheter clean and avoid the bladder infections. I've been hospitalized so many times for urosepsis, which is one of the infections that moves from the bladder to your blood, and I'm trying to maintain consistent health and not end up in the hospital again. There are a few birds chirping outside my window and their music actually begins to resonate within me and "take over" some of the pain that I'm in. Opening my computer and answering e-mails, making telephone calls to clients or friends: these are but a few things that I do each morning to put the pain in the periphery rather than have it be the center of my being.

I began to move my legs and utilize the few stomach muscles that have returned since my accident. This is the time when I truly engage life, and the morning. This is a time to get my head on straight and realize that simply being alive is an amazing gift. Don't get me wrong—it doesn't happen every morning automatically. There are times when I wake up with the flu and extra pain when it takes a little bit longer to get to the joy of being alive. But that joy, that gift is always there. And it's accessible to each and every one of us.

Fear

It's a Sunday morning with the autumn light peeking through my shades. Two more days until the 2008 election and I am scared. In a macro sense, I am scared about the turnout of the presidential election. But on the micro level, I'm scared for myself.

After winning the ESPY award presented by Oprah Winfrey, I lived three glorious years with at least one motivational speech a month. This year the economy has truly hit me as well as others in this nation. Couple this with several visits to the hospital and having to stay there for IV antibiotics for my bladder infections. I also fell out of my wheelchair in February and broke my femur. The reality of all this is that I have been unemployed and corporations aren't hiring motivational speakers. I have a small amount of money in my checking account and I am also declaring bankruptcy. The money in my checking account does not cover my bills.

I realize from my own experiences in life that I must take responsibility for the situation I'm in. From 2005 through 2007 I was finally creating a career. Having grown up with such poverty naturally when I looked at the gross amount I was making, I used my credit cards. And it seemed that I could afford it. However after realizing that there is this little thing called the net income—my yearly income became much less. Then the housing market crashed, along with much of the economy. Neither of these two aspects changes the fact that I don't have enough money in my checking account to pay my bills.

I've learned after years of challenges that when you embrace them and allow yourself to look at them, then often there is a shift and good things begin to happen. But when we are in moments of fear sometimes we just have to be fearful and not try to find the wisdom in it. Because when we are living in fear sometimes all that we can do is acknowledge it, and breathe. Breathing is one of the first things that we stop doing once we're in fear. I mean, of course our body always breathes. But the only thing that's worked for me is truly focusing on my breath. Even if it's just a few moments each day, I consciously begin breathing from my belly, allowing the air to fill up my lungs, and then exhaling slowly. When I do this a couple of times and then try and do it at some point later in the day it keeps me going and lets me know that I am alive. Breathing doesn't necessarily make me any more money but it cleanses out the constant thinking of it and lets me move through the day. I mean, let's face it—I'm already paralyzed. What good is it going to do to let my thoughts paralyze me even more?

It's another Sunday and I am at home in my bed with another bladder/kidney infection. I went to the emergency room yesterday and the silly doctor took a urine culture that will take three days to show exactly what bacteria are inside me and which of the antibiotics are sensitive to the virus. The initial results of the culture note that I do indeed have bacteria in my kidneys, however they don't know yet which antibiotics will work. Basically I know more about my body than the doctor at this point, after 15 years of dealing with these infections. He gave me a commonly used antibiotic through IV and then sent me home with the same antibiotic only one am I to take orally. The antibiotics aren't working and now I have to wait another 1-2 days to find out what is really going on. The scariest part of this process is just waiting in my bed at home feeling sicker every day and not strong enough to really advocate for my own health. I'd had so many bladder infections over the past 15 years that my veins have all but disappeared in my arms. This means that the only effective way to receive IV antibiotics is through what they call a PICC line. The line is inserted around the inside of my elbow and is moved inside near my vena cava. This could all be done on an outpatient basis with the necessary drugs and supplies ordered and then a nursing agency coming over daily to administer the antibiotics. The PICC line is a bit painful but much more effective than a regular IV port because the line is so close to my vena cava that the drugs are absorbed more readily. This process takes a couple of days to set up but at least it saves me from having to be hospitalized. With my low immune system my body is wide open to pick up other bacteria traveling throughout the hospital. For some reason I have been in the hospital here in Santa Fe at least once if not twice each month since I moved back here in December of 07. The entire process just weakens me so I never catch up to being well enough to begin working out again and actually having healthy months. It's very frustrating and yes depressing and painful. Yet somehow my experience of being alive always seems to pull me through. It can be especially difficult, when I am in extra pain due to these infections, to bring myself back to the present and just let what it is, be. At times it scares me to think about the future and what all these infections will amount up to. I realize now that even if I need to suck it up, I will have to begin looking at the University of New Mexico teaching hospital in Albuquerque. The quality of healthcare here in Santa Fe is quite simply lacking, especially when it comes to finding doctors who are also trained in paralysis. I love this town and the spirit and connections that you can make with people here who are of similar mindsets but I never figured in the amount of time I would be spending in Santa Fe's Hospital. And ultimately, this has to stop!

It seems like we all go through some sort of "bladder infection" of our own. Although the situation might be different each of us has something like this that is part of our life. I remember one day feeling so frustrated that my life was so inconsistent. And then, just a simple perspective shift allowed me to realize that actually, my life—especially my health—is consistently inconsistent. I don't know; but this realization made me feel better.

All of us have this ability. No matter what we're stuck in we can change our perspective and in one instant change our reality. In this fast-paced world where we see instant gratification, this form of changing our perspective into a new reality may be frustrating because it might not come right away. But believe me: it comes.

It's another Sunday in Santa Fe and I am just home after another week spent in the hospital. Medicare has somehow decided that during the month of October, I wasn't disabled. So they sent me no check for October. They are sending me a partial one for November but it does not arrive until December 17 and then I am back on schedule for my monthly payment. Just when it seems like I've been at my worst life does indeed get even worse. My caregiver quit last week as I was lying in bed waiting for the ambulance. I'm not sure why she quit. She and I were like brother and sister but she had concocted some strange story in her head. My dear friend Jay has been helping me since I came home from the hospital but he is leaving with his wife on Wednesday to be with relatives for Thanksgiving. So I now am without a caregiver. I'm going to make some calls tomorrow to try and set something up with a caregiving agency. Quite honestly I don't know if I have enough money in my bank account to pay for a caregiver. As far as taking care of myself, that brings up a whole other set of problems. I'm always very weak when I return from the hospital and simply getting out of bed in the morning is extremely difficult. I must admit that when I look at the situation that is occurring in my life right now I find myself breaking one of my cardinal rules: never compare myself to what I was in the past but deal with it now. But right now I am just stressed.

Today is Thanksgiving Day and it brings to mind all the little things that I am thankful for.

Two weeks ago, while waiting in bed for the ambulance to come and bring me to the hospital, my caregiver. Good and qualified caregivers are very difficult to find. My dear friend Jay was taught to be a caregiver by my old caregiver and friend, Scott. Jay and his wife Debbie have a landscaping company. So when I returned home from the hospital, even though Jay has a job, he would take the time each day to help me get out of bed use the bathroom and get dressed. However, today and his wife flew to their family for the Thanksgiving holiday and I wasn't sure what I was going to do. I'm still pretty weak from all the antibiotics and I wasn't sure about even really get myself out of bed.

And then, out of nowhere one of my other friends here in Santa Fe,

Don, showed up to help me while Jay was away. And he has been coming every morning since. What a miracle.

But then the rug was pulled out from under my life. Although I had fallen out of my wheelchair several times in the past, on this one particular morning in my loft in Santa Fe I went to open the handle of the front door. I wear clothing that is larger than my size so that it's easier to get dressed. Therefore, my right pocket hooked onto the joystick of my wheelchair and caused the wheelchair to spin around very fast, performing several 360° turns. I was thrust from the chair with such speed that I was not able to brace myself with my hands. My head and my right knee hit the tile first. My knee hurt so badly that I got finished with my bowel program with my caregiver and then lay back down in bed, figuring that I would get my knee checked out the following day.

That evening I awoke at about 2 AM and I was vomiting. Although much of my diaphragm and ability to cough has returned the only time I vomit is when my urinary tract infections are turning septic. So I called the ambulance to go to the hospital, only to find out that not only was I septic but I had broken my right femur from the fall that morning.

Apparently I had a bladder infection brewing in there and then the shock of being thrown from my wheelchair accelerated it.

Simultaneously the lease on the loft I was renting was ending. And after my bladder infection cleared up from the IV antibiotics I also had an elective surgery done. I decided to get a colostomy bag. I was just tired of the past 15 years of dealing with a 3-4 hour bowel program.

8 TRIATHLETE JIM MACLAREN DIES AT 47
From *Triathlete* magazine, August 31, 2010

Jim MacLaren (born April 13, 1963), who at one time was the world's fastest amputee triathlete, passed away Monday evening August 30th.

His life was short but amazingly impactful. After getting hit by a New York City bus while on his motorcycle back in 1985 and having his lower leg amputated below the knee, the former Yale football player reinvented himself and became the Babe Ruth of amputee athletes, running a 3:16 marathon and going 10:42 at the Ironman in Kona, Hawaii.

In June of 1993, while competing in a triathlon in Orange County, California, MacLaren was on his bike when a van went through a closed intersection, hit the back of the bike and propelled him into a pole. When he arrived at the hospital he was told that he was a quadriplegic and would never move again from the waist down.

Bob Babbitt, Jeffrey Essakow and Rick Kozlowski, three of his many friends from the sport of triathlon, created a triathlon in San

Diego after the accident to buy Jim a vehicle that he could drive with his hands. The goal was to raise $25,000 and they ended up raising $48,000 through the first-ever San Diego Triathlon Challenge. "At that event," remembers Babbitt, "a number of other amputee athletes came up to us to thank us for what we did for Jim, but to also let us know that there were so many other athletes out there that needed help. Insurance would cover a walking leg, but anything having to do with sport was considered a luxury item."

From Jim's second tragedy, the Challenged Athletes Foundation was born and in the 17 years since, CAF has raised over $28,000,000 to help disabled athletes stay in the game of life by providing grants to help purchase the equipment they need to stay in the game of life through sport.

"CAF is Jimmy's legacy," continues Babbitt. "I'm proud to say that, through the athletes that we help every day, his impact will live on forever."

ABOUT THE AUTHOR

Jennifer Hippensteel has always found words to be her release and has been writing since she was 10 years old. Her belief is that when we write from our hearts, there will always be someone out there who can relate and perhaps not feel so alone in their struggles. After losing her big brother and best friend in 2010, she was inspired to forgo her fears and publish her work to help keep her brother's spirit alive here on earth and to help her heal from the loss of a lifetime.

Mother to four exceptional spirits, Kiowa, Noah, Sage, and Maya, Jennifer resides in Lancaster County, PA, where she is a business consultant and a holistic health practitioner and Reiki master. Along with poems and short stories, Jennifer has written informative articles and content for client websites.

PHOTO CREDITS

I extend my utmost gratitude and credit to the following people and organizations for generously allowing me to use their original photos.

Cover photo. Jim modeling for physical therapy promotional calendar. Credit: Sharp Memorial Hospital, San Diego, CA.

Inside cover / Chapter 4. Jim in a promo shoot for Challenged Athletes Foundation (CAF). Credit: CAF and Tim Mantoani.

Forward. Jim as a Yale football player, circa 1994. Author's photo.

Chapter 1. Jim competing in Kona Ironman Triathlon cycling competition. Credit: Lois Schwartz.

Chapter 2. Jim competing in Kona Ironman Triathlon running competition. Credit: Lois Schwartz.

Chapter 3. Jim with Phil Bolsta, author of *Sixty Seconds: One Moment Changes Everything*. Credit: Phil Bolsta.

Chapter 4. Jim with members of the first San Diego Triathlon Challenge (SDTC), the beginning of Challenged Athletes Foundation. Credit: CAF.

Chapter 5. Jim with Emmanuel Ofosu Yeboah. Promo for CAF and *Emmanuel's Gift*. Credit CAF and Tim Mantoani.

Chapter 6. Jim with Sean O'Malley, created of Cardio Coach Guided Workouts. Credit: Karal Gregory.

Chapter 7. Jim modeling for physical therapy promotional calendar. Credit: Sharp Memorial Hospital, San Diego, CA.

Chapter 8. Jim MacLaren CAF Tribute Poster, 2010. Credit: CAF.

Fear is an exciting time.

It's our soul telling us that we need to change.

Change is powerful.

— Jim Maclaren

Made in the USA
Middletown, DE
02 February 2019